STUDY GUIDE

STOMPING OUT THE DARKNESS

FiND OuT Who YoU aRe iN ⟨...⟩
HaVe tO PuT Up WitH tHe W⟨...⟩

D0499513

Neil T. AnDeRson
aNd DaVe PaRk

Gospel Light

Published Gospel Light
Ventura, California, U.S.A.
Printed in U.S.A.

Gospel Light is an evangelical Christian publisher dedicated to serving the local church. We believe God's vision for Gospel Light is to provide church leaders with biblical, user–friendly materials that will help them evangelize, disciple and minister to children, youth and families.

It is our prayer that this book will help you discover biblical truth for your own life and help you meet the needs of others. May God richly bless you.

For a free catalog of resources from Gospel Light please contact your Christian supplier or call 1-800-4-GOSPEL.

ISBN 0-8307-1745-5
© 1995 by Neil T. Anderson and Dave Park
All rights reserved.
Printed in U.S.A.

Rights for publishing this book in other languages are contracted by Gospel Literature International (GLINT). GLINT also provides technical help for the adaptation, translation and publishing of Bible study resources and books in scores of languages worldwide. For further information, contact GLINT, P.O. Box 4060, Ontario, CA 91761-1003, U.S.A., or the publisher.

Contents

A NOTE FROM NEIL AND DAVE

In Luke 5:1-11, Jesus was instructing the multitudes from Peter's boat. "And when He had finished speaking, He said to Simon, 'Put out into the deep water and let down your nets for a catch'" (v. 4). Jesus had stopped talking, but He had not stopped teaching. Peter heard what Jesus said, but he hadn't learned until he got into the boat and put out the nets.

This study guide gives you an opportunity to get into the boat and put out the nets. You can do it alone, but we recommend that you do it with other faithful learners. It provides an opportunity for more collective wisdom, and greater learning always takes place in the context of committed relationships. Developing trusting relationships and being devoted to one another in prayer is what makes group study so enriching.

We are thankful for the tremendous work that Lisa Guest, who also developed the study guide for *The Bondage Breaker Youth Edition* (Harvest House, 1995), has done in putting together this study guide. Another helpful resource is *Busting Free!* (Gospel Light, 1994), a curriculum for teaching these truths in a Sunday School class or small group. A summary of resources available from Freedom in Christ Ministries is given at the end of this study guide.

It is our prayer that you will fully realize who you are in Christ and learn to live as a child of God. If this study guide helps make that possible, we will be thankful. May the grace and love of our heavenly Father bless you with all the riches of your inheritance in Christ.

Neil T. Anderson and Dave Park

Who Are You?

We can't point a bony finger at you, but we can and are going to ask you, "Who are you?" Start from the outside but work down to the core. Get beyond what you look like and what you do (those are good enough starting points) to who you'd still be if you lost those externals.

_____

_____

Is who we are determined by what we do—or is what we do determined by who we are? Read that question again slowly and then decide if it's one or the other or both—and explain why you think so.

_____

_____

We (Neil and Dave) think that what we do is determined by who we are, and that's why we really want you to get to know who you are in Christ. So let's get to it!

Date:_____

When the Outside and Inside Don't Add Up
(pages 18-20)

The world offers the following equations as paths to identity and meaning, to belonging and significance:

Appearance + Accomplishments + Recognition = Peace

Good looks + Popularity = Wholeness

Star performances + Great accomplishments = Happiness

Which of the above equations, if any, best describes how you're living life?

_____

_____

• When have you seen—for yourself or in a friend's life—that these equations are false? More specifically, when have you felt for yourself or seen in someone else's life that...

Appearance + Accomplishments + Recognition ≠ Peace

Good looks + Popularity ≠ Wholeness

Star performances + Great accomplishments ≠ Happiness

Success ≠ Contentment

Failure ≠ Hopelessness

The world's math is all wrong. The only identity equation that works in God's kingdom is:

You + Christ = Wholeness and Meaning

If our identity in Christ is the key to wholeness, why do you think so many believers have difficulty with self-worth, spiritual growth and maturity?

_____

_____

_____

Why would the devil want to deceive us about our true identity in Christ? What can he accomplish by keeping us down on ourselves and unsure about whether we're worth anything?

_____

_____

Too often, Satan tricks us into believing that what we do (failing, sinning) makes us what we are (failures, sinners). This false belief sinks us deeper and deeper into the muddy pit of hopelessness and defeat. The only way out of that pit is to get a grip on who you really are as God's child.

Date: _____

The Good Things We Inherited From Father Adam

(pages 21-25)

In order to understand who we really are, we need to understand what traits we inherited—good and bad—from Adam at Creation. For starters, just like Adam, we have physical bodies and inner selves, sometimes called souls, which are the parts of us created in God's image.

• Physically Alive—Like Adam, we walk around in a living, breathing earth suit made up of skin, muscle, bone, blood, fat, hair, etc.

What does 2 Corinthians 5:1-4 suggest about the relationship between your body and your soul?

_____

_____

_____

Your soul is eternal, but your body is guaranteed for only one lifetime. What does this fact say to you about your efforts to find significance through having the "right"-sized biceps or waistline, the "right" clothes and the "right" haircut?

_____

_____

_____

• Spiritually Alive—We are spiritually alive when our inner selves are united with God. After all, we were created to be in relationship with God. But Adam sinned and his relationship with God—and ours as well—was broken. That's why we were born spiritually dead and why Christ died on the cross.

When did you first become aware that you were spiritually dead? What happened in your life? What did you do after you realized your sin and your distance from God? What do you do to keep yourself close to God now?

_____

_____

_____

Maybe you're just now starting to think about your spiritual health. What sins are you becoming aware of? What emptiness are you noticing inside? If you have come to a point of recognizing that you need God's forgiveness, tell Him that. Ask Him to forgive your sins (be specific) and thank Him for sending His Son, Jesus, to pay the penalty for those sins by dying on the cross (see John 3:16). Invite Jesus to become Lord of your life and ask God to help you learn more about how to live a life that pleases Him (see Romans 10:9,10).

• Significance—We all want to be significant or important, and from the start Adam was extremely significant.

According to Genesis 1:26,27, what purpose for living did God give Adam?

_____

_____

_____

_____

Satan stole Adam's significance (and ours) when Adam sinned, but Jesus won it back for us through His death and His resurrection. Explain what Josh McDowell means when he writes, "You are 'worth Jesus' to God" (page 24 of the text).

_____

_____

_____

_____

The price that God paid for you is Jesus Christ. What purpose for living has God given you? See the "Strength Givers" at this end of this lesson.

_____

_____

_____

What does knowing that God has called you to be light and salt do to your negative thoughts about yourself?

_____

_____

• Safety and Security—Before Adam sinned in the garden, he enjoyed a sense of safety and security. He lacked nothing.

In Christ, we inherit safety and security as well as significance. What long-term safety and security does God offer you, His child? See Romans 8:38,39 and 1 John 1:9.

_____

_____

When in your day-to-day life have you felt the safety and security God gives?

_____

_____

What does Philippians 4:19 mean to you personally? (Note that Paul talks about our needs, not our wants. Those are two different lists!)

_____

_____

• Belonging—Adam and Eve experienced a sense of belonging. First Adam enjoyed an intimate relationship with God. Then, when God gave Eve to Adam—and Adam to Eve—he experienced a different sense of belonging.

When has your relationship with God, made possible because of Christ, given you a sense of belonging?

_____

_____

_____

What relationships with people give you a sense of belonging?

_____

_____

_____

How does the belonging you feel in relationships with Christian friends compare to the belonging you feel in other relationships?

_____

_____

Date: _____

The Bad Things We Inherited From Father Adam
(pages 25-32)

Just as we received good things from Adam, we also received negative side effects from his fall. Below each side effect, note evidence of this inheritance that you've found in your own life.

• Spiritual Death—When Adam and Eve sinned, they were separated from God—and that is spiritual death.

Evidence of my separation from God:

_____

_____

• Lost Knowledge of God—With their sin, Adam and Eve lost their true understanding of God as well as their ability to love God and experience a deep friendship and intimacy with Him.

Evidence of my distance from God and my inability to love Him:

_____

_____

• **Dominant Negative Emotions**—With the Fall, human beings became fearful and anxious. We also got to know shame and guilt. Depression and anger also entered the picture.

Negative emotions I struggle with:

_____

_____

_____

• **Too Many Choices**—In the Garden of Eden, Adam and Eve could make a billion good choices and only one bad choice. They made that one bad choice (and you and I probably would have done the same thing!), and that means we're confronted every day with a ton of good and bad choices.

Some of the countless decisions I face each day—and some of the bad choices I make:

_____

_____

_____

• **Attributes Become Needs**—Another long-term effect of sin is that our three glowing strengths before the Fall became three glaring needs after the Fall. Acceptance was replaced by rejection, and so we have a need to belong. Innocence was replaced by guilt and shame, and so we need our self-worth to be restored. Authority was replaced by weakness and helplessness, and so we have a need for strength and self-control.

Evidence that I need to belong, that I fear rejection, that I know what peer pressure feels like:

_____

_____

Evidence that I have a poor self-image, that I need a sense of self-worth:

_____

_____

_____

Evidence that I want some control:

_____

_____

_____

• Sinful behavior is a wrong attempt to meet our basic needs. Are you allowing God to meet your needs or are you looking to the world to meet your needs? It's an issue of relationship and maturity. The better we understand our identity in Christ, the more we will grow in maturity. And the more mature we become, the easier it will be for us to choose what is right.

What choices of what is right have become easier for you as you've become more mature as a person and/or as a Christian?

_____

_____

_____

What choices are still tough for you? Pray about those situations and, if you're brave, have a friend pray for you, too.

_____

_____

A quick review: Your true identity is not based on what you do or what you have, but on who you are in Christ. That's what we'll be working on here—getting through our thick skulls who we are in Christ! After all, Jesus Christ came after Adam and won back for us the spiritual life Adam and Eve lost. The triumph of Jesus and what it has gained for us is the theme of the next chapter.

Start Stomping!

Shout Down the World

Grab a bunch of magazines and cut out ads that tell you who you "should" be. Make a collage (that means glue them on a piece of paper) and then, with a Christian friend, consider the message. (The silliness of the message just might make you laugh.) Does what the world say you should be really matter in the big (eternal) scheme of things?

Who Are You?

Say, "Thanks!"

Who has been there for you when you didn't feel you "belonged"? Does that person know you appreciate him or her? Send a note, give a flower, buy a piece of pizza at lunch—let that person know (in so many words or just by actions) that you appreciate the friendship!

Reach Out and Touch Someone

Where can you reach out and offer your friendship to someone who may need the sense of belonging that you've experienced? Pray aloud.

> Okay, God, I see what I've inherited from Adam and Eve, and it's not pretty. You know, it's real hard to deal with being down on myself, with loneliness, with the inability to make good choices, with anger and depression and shame and guilt and fear. I don't want to hide from You or anyone else, but sometimes it's hard not to. God, help me hear Your truth. Help me really hear that You love me. And help me get to know You better. I pray in Jesus' name. Amen.

Strength Givers

These words are *for* you and *about* you! As you read each day's verse, ask yourself, "How would my life be different if I could live out this truth?"—and ask God to help you do so.

Monday—Matthew 5:13
Tuesday—Matthew 5:14
Wednesday—Acts 1:8
Thursday—John 15:16
Friday—Ephesians 3:1

ER TWO

Forever Different

What did you learn from the story of Tank and Turk and the Bimbo twins?

_____

_____

Tank and Turk, those bundles of physical urges, sure behaved differently than Tank and Turk, the lean, mean, running machines. Why?

_____

_____

Think about your perception of yourself. Are you more like Tank and Turk before the track coach discovered them or Tank and Turk after they started working out? Explain your answer.

_____

_____

Many Christians—and you may be one of them—are not enjoying the victory and freedom that is their inheritance in Christ because they have inaccurate ideas about themselves. If we don't know what God says about us and who we are in Christ, we will suffer from a poor self-image. We must get a handle on our true identity in Christ and lose our old identity in sinful Adam.

Date: _____

The Life-changing Difference of Being in Christ
(pages 35-37)

Have you put your trust in Christ? Then, from God's perspec-

17

tive, you are no longer identified with Adam and his sin, but with Jesus and His righteousness. Are you identifying with Him, though?

_____

_____

• Unending Dependence on God—Adam depended on God to a point, but Jesus was completely dependent on God the Father.

On a scale from Adam up to Jesus, evaluate your dependence on God. How well do you do in general?

_____

_____

In what aspects of your life are you most independent of God? Why?

_____

_____

What does the world—our society and your school campus— teach about dependence and independence? Which is acceptable in the world's eyes and which is not? How does God figure into the world's message?

_____

_____

• Uninterrupted Spiritual Life—Both Adam and Jesus were born spiritually alive. Adam died spiritually when he sinned, but Jesus never gave up His spiritual life because He never sinned. If you've accepted Christ as your Savior, you are no longer spiritually dead but alive in Him now and forever.

Because of Adam, you were born spiritually dead, and sin continues to interfere with your Christian walk. What specific things tend to interrupt your spiritual life these days?

_____

_____ Forever Different

What does it mean to you to pray, "Lead us not into temptation"?

_____

_____

What can you learn about resisting temptation from Jesus in Matthew 4:1-11?

_____

_____

The differences between Adam and Jesus spell the difference between life and death for you and me. Read on!

Date: _____

WHAT A DIFFERENCE CHRIST'S DIFFERENCE MAKES IN US!
(pages 37-41)

In 1 Corinthians 15:22, Paul writes, "As in Adam all die, so also in Christ all shall be made alive." Believers are "in Christ," and being in Christ is the most important part of our identity.

• New Life Requires New Birth—We weren't born in Christ. We were born in sin (see Psalm 51:5). So what is God's plan for transforming us from being in Adam to being in Christ? His plan is for spiritual birth.

What did you learn about your spiritual life in Christ from the comparison of physical birth to spiritual rebirth (page 38 of the text)?

_____

_____

You may have come across a couple mindblowers in the text. We're thinking of the statements "Eternal life is not something you get when you die" and "Salvation is not a future addition; it's a present transformation" (see John 17:3; 2 Corinthians 5:17). In plain English, what do these facts mean to you?

_____

_____

• New Life Brings New Identity—Being a Christian is not just a matter of getting something; it's a matter of being someone. Being born again changed you into someone who didn't exist before. So what you get from God as His child isn't the point; it's who you are. And it's not what you do as a Christian that determines who you are; it's who you are that determines what you do. More mindblowers, right? Let's untangle them.

If you think you're no good, you'll probably live like you're no good. Could this be your motto? In what ways are you living like you're no good?

_____

_____

Do you see yourself as a child of God? Where in your life are you living in victory and freedom as Christ did?

_____

_____

If you find yourself living as if you're no good more than you live according to the truth that you are a child of God, Satan may be one reason. What can you do to protect yourself from Satan's deception about your relationship to God and your value to Him? (We started your answer for you! That's just the kind of writers we are!)

1. Read this book.
2. Do the "Start Stomping" activities.
3. _____
4. _____
5. _____

• New Life Results in a New Title—The Bible says we are saints because God calls us saints (see Ephesians 1:1; Philippians 1:1).

What kind of person do you think of when you hear the word "saint"? Who comes to mind?

Forever Different

_____

_____

What do you think about being called a saint yourself? How does that make you feel? How do you think God intends that title to make you feel?

_____

_____

If you think of yourself as a sinner, how will you probably act? Give three or four examples from a typical day.

_____

_____

As a child of God, you are a saint who unfortunately happens to sin, sometimes several times a day. But if you were to think of yourself as a saint, how would you act in some of the circumstances you just outlined?

_____

_____

You've heard it before and now you'll hear it again! What you do doesn't determine who you are; who you are determines what you do. Got that, Saint?

Date: _____

What Is True of Christ Is True of You
(pages 41-44)

Yep, you read that right. What is true of Jesus now applies to you because you are *in* Christ. It's part of your identity.

• Review the "Who Am I?" list that begins on page 41 of the text. (Some you'll recognize from last chapter's "Strength Givers.") If you are in Christ, every one of these statements is completely true of you. They aren't true because of anything you've done. They're true because of what Jesus has done for you.

Which one or two of these "Who Am I?" statements are the most encouraging to you today? Why?

_____

_____

_____

Which one or two of these "Who Am I?" statements are the most challenging to you today? Why?

_____

_____

Which one or two of these "Who Am I?" statements are the hardest for you to believe? Why?

_____

_____

You can make all these traits you just read about more meaningful and productive in your life by simply choosing to believe what God has said about you. Believing what God says about you doesn't make it true. What God says about you is true and therefore you believe it.

Date: _____

The Bright Hope of Being a Child of God
(pages 44-46)

As the helpless and hopeless children of sinful Adam, there was nothing about us to make us acceptable to God. But through Jesus, God provided the only way for us to become part of His family. You are no longer a spiritual orphan; you are a child of God.

• As a Christian, you are someone very special.

Who did what to give you that special status?

_____

_____

Read 1 John 3:1-3. What hope do you find in this description of God's love and its effect on your life?

Forever Different

_____

_____

_____

We are children of God—now! When we believe that, we begin to live like the children of God we are. But we must see ourselves as children of God in order to live like children of God.

• Just in case you weren't ready to accept the invitation earlier, we'll extend it again. Would you like to become a child of God? Are you ready to receive Jesus into your life (see John 1:12)? Let God know of your choice by saying the following prayer:

> Lord Jesus, I need You. Thank You for dying on the cross for my sins. I believe that You were resurrected from the dead in order that I might have spiritual life. I put my trust for eternal life in You and invite You into my life to be my Lord and Master. I no longer want to live independently of You. Thank You for giving me eternal life. In Jesus' name I pray. Amen.

START STOMPING!

CELEBRATE DEPENDENCE DAY!

In the Old Testament, God's people would build altars to remind them of God's faithfulness. With some small stones, build an altar. (Or, if you prefer, draw a picture.) Then on an index card write down the instance(s) of God's faithfulness this altar is commemorating. As you dedicate this altar, ask God to forgive your independence and to teach you greater dependence on Him.

POSTER TIME

Get a piece of poster board and then get creative! Use marking pens, pictures from magazines, Bible references, Christian symbols and old photographs to do whatever it takes to illustrate and get into your brain the truth: "What I do doesn't determine who I am; who I am determines what I do—and I am a child of God!"

EARS TO HEAR

Just in case you didn't do what the text strongly encouraged you to do, we'll invite you once again to read aloud the "Who Am I?" list. Yep—out loud! And stick your name into those statements, too, for greater impact ("I, Poindexter, am a child of God." "I, Esmerelda, am a new person. My past is forgiven and everything is new.").

> God, it's hard to get my mind around all You've done for me. Through the death of Your Son, Jesus, You've made it possible for me to be Your child. All I've had to do is accept Your invitation. Thank You for helping me hear and respond to that invitation. Now, God, please help me learn how to live as Your child. I pray in Jesus' name. Amen.

STRENGTH GIVERS

These words are *for* you and *about* you! As you read each day's verse, ask yourself, "How would my life be different if I could live out this truth?"—and ask God to help you do so.

Monday—1 Corinthians 1:30
Tuesday—John 1:12
Wednesday—2 Corinthians 5:17
Thursday—Ephesians 1:1
Friday—1 Peter 2:9,10

See Yourself for Who You Really Are

What does my (Neil's) account of Claire teach you?

_____

_____

What was Claire's "secret"?

_____

_____

Claire accepted herself for who God said she was in Christ—His child. She also confidently committed herself to God's main goal for her life—to be like Christ and to love people. Can you say the same about yourself?

_____

_____

• Our guess is that, like most Christians and unlike Claire, you struggle to accept who you are. You don't simply accept yourself as a child of God. We'd also guess that, unlike Claire, you find it hard to be focused primarily on God's call to be like Christ and love other people.

What keeps you from being more like Claire?

_____

_____

Claire's experience reminds us how important it is to base our Christian lives on what we believe instead of how we behave. We need a firm grip on what God says about who we are before we will experience much success at living the Christian life.

Date: _____

BELIEF BEFORE BEHAVIOR
(pages 48-55)

A healthy Christian lifestyle is the result of a healthy Christian belief system, not the other way around. If what we believe about God and ourselves is shaky, then our day-to-day behavior will be shaky.

• Get a Grip on God's Grace—"Grace" is one of those words you may have heard a lot but no one's ever really defined, and you've never asked because you felt you should already know what it means! Well, a classic definition of grace is "unmerited favor." Grace is goodness we receive that we don't deserve and couldn't earn. It's God's gift of forgiveness and eternal life through the death of His Son, Jesus.

Remember Myndee Hudson? What about her story hit you the hardest? Be specific.

_____

_____

_____

What has happened in your life to help you realize what's really important?

_____

_____

_____

To quote Myndee, "When you know you're going to die, you only care about things that are going to last. Before I was sick, Jesus was only a part of my life. Now He's everything to me." Is Jesus only a part of your life? Or is He everything to you? What do your answers tell you about yourself and how you're living life?

See Yourself for Who You Really Are

Getting right with God means settling once and for all the issue that God is your loving Father. You are a child of God, you are created in His image, and you have been declared righteous by Him because you have put your trust in Christ.

When you shift your focus away from your identity as God's child and try to be something you're not or wish you were someone else, you'll struggle. What interferes with your focus on the truth that you are God's child?

Read again these powerful truths: We don't serve God to gain His acceptance; we are accepted, so we serve God. We don't follow Him in order to be loved; we are loved, so we follow Him. What are you doing to earn God's acceptance? What are you doing to earn His love?

Make your answers to the two previous questions the topic of a prayer. Ask God to remove the barriers to your belief that you are His child. Ask Him to free you from feeling you have to earn His acceptance and love. And ask Him to protect you from Satan's efforts to convince you that you are unworthy and will always be unacceptable to God.

Remember—you are a saint whom God has declared righteous. Believing this truth about your identity will set you free.

• The Fallout from God's Grace—God's grace has far-reaching effects on our lives, as the list of truths that begins on page 52 of the text suggests. Review this "Since I am in Christ, by the grace of God..." list.

Which one or two of these "Since I am in Christ" statements are the most encouraging to you today? Why?

_____

_____

_____

Which one or two of these "Since I am in Christ" statements are the most challenging to you today? Why?

_____

_____

_____

Which one or two of these "Since I am in Christ" statements are the hardest for you to believe? Why?

_____

_____

Understanding who you are in Christ won't change the circumstances of your life. But your perception of your identity makes a big difference in your success at dealing with the challenges and conflicts that come your way.

Date: _____

There's a Difference Between Relationship and Fellowship
(pages 55-57)

What can you do to change your relationship with your heavenly Father? (Yes, this is a trick question.)

_____

_____

What can you do to affect how well you get along with your heavenly Father? Think about your relationship to your earthly father or to my (Neil's) relationship to my father.

_____

_____

You are a child of God—period. There's absolutely nothing you can do to make yourself more a child of God. But you can enjoy a more harmonious relationship with God if you diligently try to obey Him.

Date: _____

Believe What You Perceive in Others
(pages 57-60)

Miss Thompson learned an important lesson from Teddy Stallard. What did Miss Thompson and Teddy teach you about how we are to treat other people?

_____

_____

_____

As important as it is for you to believe in your true identity as a child of God, it is equally important that you see other Christians for who they are and treat them the way they should be treated. Gulp! Okay, who in the course of your week could you have treated more like the child of God that they are?

_____

_____

_____

Write out Ephesians 4:29.

_____

_____

_____

When you blew it, who has given you grace through his or her words? Who has loved you no matter what you did or didn't do?

_____

_____

Who can you, a new recruit for God's construction crew, build up through your words today? Do it!

Date: _____

BELIEVING THE TRUTH ABOUT YOURSELF
(pages 60-62)

• Remember Jenny? At what stage of Jenny's transformation are you right now? Are you...

Depressed, wondering where to turn?

_____

_____

Waiting for someone to affirm your value to God?

_____

_____

Beginning to understand the truth that you are a child of God, no better and no worse than any other of His children?

_____

_____

_____

Walking by faith, seeing yourself for who you really are in Christ?

_____

_____

Wherever you see yourself along this time line from Jenny's life, think about where you want to be. What goals do you have for your walk of faith? Choose one goal and identify the next step you will take toward reaching that goal. Now take that step!

See Yourself for Who You Really Are

_____

_____

_____

You are a righteous, accepted child of God—and that is solid truth from the Bible. Read and reread the identity statements listed in the second and third chapters of the text. See yourself in them. Believe them Walk in them. As you walk by faith, your behavior as a Christian will begin to conform to what you believe.

Start Stomping!

This Test Could Change Your Life

Take the test that I (Dave) challenged Kristy to take, and see what happens. Read aloud the "Since I am in Christ" statements and really listen to what God is saying to you about you.

Tune-Up Time!

How harmonious is your relationship with God right now? Disobedience means disharmony. Where are you being disobedient? 'Fess up! Receive forgiveness! Enjoy harmony with God.

Find a Friend

Living a Christian life isn't easy, so don't try to do it alone. Find a friend—someone who knows the Lord and has walked closely with Him for a good while—and let this person know where you're at and what you need. Do you need affirmation and encouragement like Jenny did? Do you struggle to believe you're valuable to God? Do you need help obeying God's commands in a certain area of your life? Do you need prayer? Let this person give you the support you need. Give him or her the opportunity to be an active member of God's construction crew.

God, I feel like the father who wanted Jesus to heal his
sick boy (see Mark 9:14-27). Like that dad who believed
You could heal his son, I believe You can help me. But
also like that dad who said, "If you can do anything...," I
need help with my unbelief. I believe, God, that I am
Your child. Help my unbelief. Amen.

STRENGTH GIVERS

These words are for you and about you! As you read each day's
verse, ask yourself, "How would my life be different if I could live
out this truth?"—and ask God to help you do so.

Monday—1 Corinthians 6:19,20
Tuesday—2 Corinthians 5:21
Wednesday—Ephesians 1:4
Thursday—Ephesians 1:7,8
Friday—Romans 5:1

Something Old, Something New

What's the difference between being a saint who sins rather than being a sinner? It's more than just playing with words. Give an example or two of how the difference can affect your thoughts and behavior.

_____

_____

_____

Our position in Christ is settled and solid, but our daily actions, often marked by failures and disobedience, disturb the harmony of our relationships with God.

Read Romans 7:19,24. What good do you want to do that you can't seem to do? What wrong that you don't want to do, do you find yourself doing anyway?

_____

_____

_____

Your answer to the preceding question points to the biggest problem for us Christians—the sinful side of our sainthood. The more we understand about our old sinful selves, our new selves in Christ and the sin we can't seem to shake, the better prepared we will be to grow in our identity in Christ.

Date: _____

From Sinner to Saint
(pages 65-68)

First review the truth. What do the following verses say about you who have accepted Jesus as your Lord and Savior?

Romans 8:9

_____

_____

2 Corinthians 5:17

_____

_____

Ephesians 5:8

_____

_____

Colossians 1:13

_____

_____

We have changed kingdoms: we are members of God's kingdom, not Satan's. When we first trusted Christ, the darkness departed and we are now light. We are not partly new and partly old with two creatures inside battling for supremacy. But still we struggle with Satan's temptations, darkness and the old self...

Remember the story of Eustace in C. S. Lewis's *Voyage of the Dawn Treader* (summarized on pages 65 and 66 of the text)? What does Eustace's transformation tell you about your change from sinner to saint?

_____

_____

_____

If you believe you are part dragon and part human, you will live an unfruitful life. When God took away your sin, He cut away your dragon skin (and dragon heart) and you became a totally new creature. Learning to think and act like a new creature in Christ (the outer change called "sanctification") continues throughout life. But learning to live successfully like a new creature will only happen when you accept the truth that you already are a new creature.

Something Old, Something New

• The Nature of the Matter—Before you came to Christ, you were dead in sin, subject to Satan's power, and living completely to fulfill sinful lusts and desires (see Ephesians 2:1-3). When you came into relationship with God through your new birth, you didn't add a new divine nature to your old sinful nature. You exchanged natures (see 2 Corinthians 5:17).

What evidence do you see in your life and in your heart that you have indeed exchanged natures? Where have you had glimpses of your new divine nature?

_____

_____

_____

Why is having that new divine nature essential to being able to grow in your relationship with the Lord and become more Christlike?

_____

_____

_____

• Either One or the Other—Ephesians 5:8 reads, "You were formerly darkness, but now you are light in the Lord; walk as children of light."

What's the difference between being darkness and being *in* darkness? What does this tell you about yourself before you knew Jesus?

_____

_____

What's the difference between being light and being *in* light? What does this tell you, a believer, about your role in the world?

_____

_____

_____

What instruction follows the statement that you are light—and what does that command mean in terms of your everyday life?

_____

_____

In the coming chapters, we'll look more closely at what it means to walk by faith and walk in the Spirit. Right now, though, consider how crucial it is that you have the nature of Christ in you.

With Christ's nature within, you can *be* like Christ, not just *act* like Him. In what areas of your life today do you most need to be like Christ, not just act like Him? Let God know that's where you need His transforming touch.

God knows we can't measure up to His standards on our own, so He gives us an entirely new self—the life of Christ in us. This astounding act of grace enables us to become the people God wants us to be.

Date: _____

Is the "Old Man" Alive, Dying or Already Dead?

(pages 68-71)

Before we came to Christ, we were sinners because it was our natures —our old selves, our "natural" ways—to sin. We couldn't accept or understand the things of the Spirit.

• Rest in Peace—At salvation, your old inner self died by crucifixion with Christ (see Romans 6:6; Galatians 2:20).

Your old self (the sinner) and your old nature (sinfulness) died with Christ on the cross and are gone forever. Does that mean you are now sinless? Support your answer with specific evidence from your life.

_____

_____

_____

Something Old, Something New

Sin and Satan are still around, and they are strong and appealing. But because of the crucifixion of the old self, sin's power over us is broken. We are no longer under any obligation to serve sin, to obey sin or to respond to sin.

> We sin when we make a willful decision to allow ourselves to act independently of God (which is how our old self acted all the time!). What decisions from the past seven days came to mind as you read that definition of sin? Let God know you're aware of those decisions to act independently of Him and ask His forgiveness (see 1 John 1:9).

_____

_____

_____

When we make the wrong decision to act independently of God, we violate our new natures and our new identity. Such actions must be confessed and turned away from.
• Once Dead, Always Dead—Colossians 3:3 begins with the words "for you have died." Paul is describing what has happened, not telling you something you need to do.

> Where, if at all, are you—like the pastor who visited me (Neil)—struggling to let your old self die?

_____

_____

_____

God expects you to know, accept and believe that your old self has died and been replaced by a new self, controlled by a new nature.

What freedom comes with accepting this truth?

_____

_____

_____

The new life that characterizes your new self is nothing less than the life of Jesus Christ implanted in you. The old self is dead, once and for all.

Date: _____

Where Does the Flesh Fit into the Picture?
(pages 71-73)

As my (Neil's) Navy experience reflects, when we're programmed to react a certain way under one skipper's authority, it takes time to get used to a new skipper. Yep, we're talking about the old self who operated under the authority of sin (the old skipper) and the new self who is in Christ (your new skipper).

• Reacting to Your Old Skipper—Our old sinful selves with their sinful natures were cruel, self-serving skippers under the authority of Satan himself. By God's grace, we have a new admiral—Jesus—and a new skipper: our new selves are powered by the divine nature of Jesus Christ. So why do we live as if our old skippers are still in control? Because everything we learned before we became Christians was programmed into our brains.

What habits and patterns of thinking that you learned from the world still influence how you act?

_____

_____

In what areas of your life do you especially tend to operate independently of God and center your interests on yourself?

_____

_____

When you were born again, your old self died and your new self came to life. But your flesh (your previously learned independence) remained. So even though your old skipper is gone, your flesh remains in opposition to God as a programmed tendency for sin—living independently of God.

• Responding to Your New Skipper—As a Christian you are no longer "in the flesh" or spiritually dead. You are in Christ. But even though you are not *in* the flesh, you may still choose to walk *according* to the flesh (see Romans 8:12,13). You may still act independently of God by saying yes to the patterns and habits programmed into your mind by the world you lived in.

> It's your responsibility to keep the flesh and its deeds from dominating your life. How well are you doing that? If you're experiencing success, what's your secret? If you're struggling, try to figure out why.

> _____

> _____

How can you keep the flesh from dominating your life? First, by learning to walk in the Spirit (see Galatians 5:16) and, second, by letting God transform your pattern of thinking by "the renewing of your mind" (Romans 12:2). And those two topics are the focus of the next five chapters. (Yes, five! This is important stuff!) But first a few more things about sin and sainthood.

Date: _____

What Role Does Sin Play in Our Struggle Toward Saintly Behavior?
(pages 73-76)

When you received Christ, the power of sin to dominate you was broken. You no longer have to sin, but sin still strongly appeals to your flesh, tempting you to act independently of God. It is your responsibility to not let sin reign in your life (see Romans 6:12,13).

• Doing What I Don't Want to Do—We're back to recognizing once again, with Paul, that we know what we should be doing, but we can't do it (see Romans 7:15,16).

According to Romans 7:20, why can't you and I do what we know we should be doing?

_____

_____

_____

What did you learn about yourself and the sin living in you from the comparison of sin to a sliver in your finger (page 75 of the text)?

_____

_____

• On the Battleground—Now let's look at where the struggle to do what you want to do takes place.

According to Romans 7:22,23, where does your desire to do what's right come from? And where does sin attack in an attempt to keep you from doing right?

_____

_____

_____

Where do these opponents—your new self and your flesh—wage war? What kind of defensive strategy does that location suggest to you?

_____

_____

The battleground between your new self (your inner being) and your flesh (your previously learned independence) is your mind. That's why it is so important for you to learn how to renew your mind (see Romans 12:2) and take every thought captive to the obedience of Christ (see 2 Corinthians 10:5). So stay tuned—and remember that, thanks to God, the battle for your mind is a winnable war.

Start Stomping!

Something Old,
Something New

A Little Help From a Friend

Sometimes we are the last to notice any changes or growth in ourselves because we live with ourselves day in and day out. It may be hard for you to identify any changes in your life and in your heart since you named Jesus your Lord and exchanged natures. So ask a friend or two what changes they have seen and are seeing in you as you continue along your Christian walk.

Bon Voyage, Skipper

Get together with a close friend or two from church and have a farewell party for the old skipper. That means good food and plenty of it as you talk about the old skipper and celebrate his or her departure. Share your lists of those habits and patterns of thinking that each of you learned from the world and that still influence how you act. Let each other know those areas of your life where you tend to operate independently of God and center your interests on yourself. Then, as a way of saying farewell to these things, agree to ask each other from time to time how life under the new skipper is. This will remind you that the old skipper is in fact gone and encourage you to respond only to the new skipper.

Drive Defensively!

Okay, the opponents have been identified and the battleground located. The war between your new self (your inner being) and your flesh (your previously learned independence) occurs in your mind. Before we get to the five chapters on how to win the war, ask some Christian friends (ideally, some folks who've been dealing with this battle for a lot longer than you have) what they do to stand strong in the Lord and resist the appeals of the flesh, their old skippers. No need to wait until the next chapter to start driving defensively!

> God, I could have written those words that Paul said—I do what I don't want to do and I don't do what I want to do. And sometimes it's awfully easy to act independently of You. I had a lot of practice doing that! I'm glad this chapter reminded me that this struggle against

independence and sin is a winnable war. I'm sure anxious to learn how to win. Help me stand strong in You against the appeal of sin, that old skipper I know too well. Thanks. I pray in Jesus' name. Amen.

Strength Givers

These words are *for* you and *about* you! As you read each day's verse, ask yourself, "How would my life be different if I could live out this truth?"—and ask God to help you do so.

Monday—Romans 6:1-6
Tuesday—1 Thessalonians 5:5
Wednesday—Galatians 2:20
Thursday—1 Corinthians 3:16
Friday—1 John 3:1,2

Becoming the Spiritual Person You Want to Be

Think of someone in whom you see Christ. Why does that person come to mind? What about that person reminds you of Christ?

_____

_____

I (Dave) received the compliment of a lifetime when the Kenyan soldiers told their commander they saw Christ in me. What does it take to be a Christian in whom others can see Christ daily? What will move us away from selfishness and fleshly desires to loving service to God and others? Any ideas at this point?

_____

_____

_____

If people are to see Christ in our lives, we first need a firm grip on our identity in Christ. We need to accept the reality that, since we are in Christ, His divine nature is part of us. Second, we must begin to renew our minds and retrain the flesh. This living out our true identity in Christ is called walking in the Spirit. Let's look at some of Scripture's guidelines for doing so.

Date: _____

THREE PERSONS AND THE SPIRIT
(pages 80-86)

In 1 Corinthians 2:14—3:3, Paul talks about three kinds of people: the natural person, the spiritual person and the fleshly person. Let's look at each closely.

• The Natural Person—The natural person is spiritually dead, separated from God, living independently from God. The natural person can't help but sin.

Review the description of the natural person and the accompanying chart (pages 80-82 of the text). Where do you see your old self under the old skipper?

_____

_____

_____

List some of the specific changes in your body, emotions, will, mind and purpose since you named Jesus as Lord. What have you left behind? What don't you struggle with as much anymore? Thank God for His transforming work in your life.

_____

_____

_____

• The Spiritual Person—The spiritual person has been transformed. When he accepted Christ, his spirit was united with God's Spirit. He now enjoys forgiveness of sin, acceptance in God's family and the knowledge that he is worth something.

How did you react to the description of the spiritual person (pages 82-84)? Was it encouraging? Discouraging? Both? Why?

_____

_____

List some of the specific characteristics of body, emotions, will, mind and purpose that you want God to bring about in you. Ask Him to show you how to cooperate with Him in His transforming work so that you can become more mature in Christ and make better choices more consistently.

_____

_____

_____

• The Fleshly Person—The fleshly person is a Christian—spiritually alive in Christ and declared righteous by God—but that's where the similarity ends. Instead of being directed and controlled by the Spirit, this believer chooses to follow the temptations of his flesh.

Where, if at all, do you unfortunately see yourself in the description of the fleshly person (pages 84-86 of the text)?

_____

_____

_____

Why do so many of us believers live so far below our potentials in Christ? One reason is that we forget who we are in Christ, so we don't actively apply that truth to our daily walks. Also, we don't realize how much Satan tries to block our growth and maturity as God's children.

_____

_____

_____

Which of these reasons—and maybe some other reasons as well—contribute to your tendencies to be a fleshly person? Confess those aloud to God and ask for His help.

_____

_____

_____

Date:_____

GUIDELINES FOR THE SPIRIT-FILLED WALK
(pages 86-94)

Know at the start that there isn't any magic formula for walking in the
Spirit. Walking according to the Spirit is more like a relationship with
a good friend than a list of do's and don'ts.
• What the Spirit-walk Is Not—The Spirit-filled walk is neither
license (totally disregarding God's loving guidelines and doing whatever you want) nor legalism (obeying a bunch of do's and don'ts).
Being led by the Spirit means you are free to do the right thing and
to live a responsible life.

> First, consider the results of license. When have you learned
> from experience that God's loving guidelines exist to protect
> you? Asked differently, when have you made a poor decision
> and been in bondage to the consequences of your choice?

_____

_____

_____

God's laws are designed to protect you, not tie you down and stran-
gle you. Your real freedom is your ability to choose to live obediently
within the protective guidelines God has given.

> Now think about legalism. When has your response to some-
> one laying down the law been the immediate desire to cross
> that line and perhaps actually crossing it?

_____

_____

_____

> When it comes to a Spirit-filled walk, demanding good things
> (Bible study, prayer, regular church attendance and witnessing)
> is no more effective than forbidding bad things. What's

happened when you've approached these good things as "shoulds" or "have to's" rather than as the means to a closer relationship to Jesus?

_____

_____

_____

God's law—those rules for behavior we find in the Bible—is a necessary, protective standard and guideline. When we live within that law, we are free to develop a spirit-to-Spirit relationship with God (see 1 Corinthians 6:17; 2 Corinthians 3:5,6).

• What the Spirit-filled Walk Is—Again, the Spirit-filled walk is neither license nor legalism, but liberty. It's the freedom to be who we already are in Christ: loved and accepted children of God. And our freedom in Christ is freedom to choose whether to walk according to the Spirit or according to the flesh.

Why is it key that we are to walk in the Spirit and not sit? What does the action of walking suggest to you?

_____

_____

_____

Why is it key that we are to walk in the Spirit and not run? Again, what does the action of walking as opposed to running suggest to you?

_____

_____

_____

We are to walk, not be sitting in idle and letting our mind coast in neutral. And we are to walk, not be running in an effort to achieve the Spirit-filled life through endless, exhausting activity.

When are you tempted to sit back and not move?

_____

_____

In what circumstances do you tend to run ahead and try to achieve the Spirit-filled life through lots of activity?

_____

_____

_____

Read Matthew 11:28-30. In your own words, explain what this image says about the Spirit-filled life, its pace and how to live it. Comment, too, on what this image says about how God chooses to get things done in the world.

_____

_____

_____

The yoke that Jesus offers means a restful walk with Him. And that picture of walking in the Spirit with Jesus points out that God has chosen to work in partnership with you to do His work in the world today. As remarkable as it sounds, neither Jesus nor you will accomplish much unless both of you pull your side of the yoke.

• Walking by Being Led—Walking according to the Spirit is also a matter of being led by the Spirit (see Romans 8:14). Consider the following two-part truth and what it means for you.

"God won't *make* you walk in the Spirit."—What does this statement say to you about your freedom and your responsibility as a child of God?

_____

_____

_____

"And the devil *can't* make you walk in the flesh."—What does this statement say to you about your freedom of choice and your ability to stand strong against Satan's efforts to draw you away from God?

_____

_____

The Spirit-walk is one of being led, not driven, and it is your choice to follow either the leading of the Spirit or the desires of the flesh.
• The Proof Is in the Fruit—How can you know if you're being led by the Spirit or the flesh? By looking at your behavior, and Galatians 5 gives us some standards by which we can evaluate our attitudes and actions.

Read Galatians 5:19-21. What kinds of attitudes and behaviors suggest that a person is walking according to the flesh?

_____

_____

_____

Read Galatians 5:22,23. What kinds of attitudes and behaviors suggest that a person is following the Spirit's leading?

_____

_____

Walking according to the Spirit is a moment-by-moment, day-by-day experience. When you step off the path of the Spirit, confess and renounce your sin to God and anyone you may have offended, receive forgiveness, and return to the right path.

A few things about confession. First, to whom do you need to confess when you've made a wrong choice? (See pages 92 and 93 in the text.)

_____

_____

_____

Second, keep in mind that your role as a Christian is to model growth, not perfection. How does confession model and even encourage growth?

_____

_____

In Christ, you are free from the power of sin. But if Satan can convince you that you're not free, you'll remain in captivity. The more you walk in step with Jesus, the better prepared you'll be to recognize Satan's deception and disarm his strategy.

Start Stomping!

Grab Those Scissors!

It's time to be creative! Make a collage, a drawing or a poster that will remind you of what a Spirit-filled walk is and maybe even isn't. Illustrate the truth of Matthew 11:28-30. Use the universal "no" sign: draw a slash through those words and/or pictures that communicate what the Spirit-filled walk is not. Whatever you do, make it a powerful encouragement to live the kind of life you want to be living.

Yep, It's a Step of Faith

Find a blindfold and a friend. Cover your eyes with the blindfold and have your friend lead you around for five minutes. Pay attention to what you're thinking and feeling as you walk along. After five minutes, switch roles. Now as you lead your blindfolded friend along, notice again your thoughts and feelings. What does this exercise teach you about walking the Spirit-filled walk? What do being led and leading help you understand about God, the One who wants to lead you? Extra-Credit Question: Jesus is a far more reliable, patient and available guide than either you or your friend—and that's good news, isn't it? What can—and will—you do to be more sensitive to His leading? How can the Bible help you?

Get Those Hands Dirty

Remember back in elementary school when you first saw an avocado pit sprout roots and little green leaves? There's something awesome about watching something grow—and there's also much to be learned. So plant something—a single seed, a row of vegetables, a tiny plant. Yes, you'll have to do some work to keep it alive, but as you work to keep it growing, think of yourself as the seed and God as your gardener, and let your little plant encourage you in your own growth in the Lord. He's doing the work for your growth. Like your little plant, you just need to receive all He wants to give you that will help you grow in Him.

God, I get uncomfortable looking at the kind of person You want me to be and realizing the kind of person I usually am. That description of the spiritual person seems pretty unreachable, and the description of the fleshly person sure makes me squirm. I'm glad You give me guidelines for how to live the kind of life I want to live for You. It helped me to see that walking with You isn't license or legalism. Help me get to know Your voice better so that I can recognize it easily, and give me the strength I need to make the right choice to follow Your Spirit's leading and not the desires of the flesh. Amen.

Becoming the Spiritual Person You Want to Be

STRENGTH GIVERS

These words are *for* you and *about* you! As you read each day's verse, ask yourself, "How would my life be different if I could live out this truth?"—and ask God to help you do so.

Monday—1 Corinthians 2:16
Tuesday—1 John 5:18
Wednesday—Colossians 1:14
Thursday—Colossians 1:27
Friday—2 Timothy 1:7

The Power of Positive Believing

The adventure film *Indiana Jones and the Last Crusade* offers us a poor picture of faith as Indy steps off a ledge for what appeared to be a long deadly fall. Instead, after only a few feet, he lands on a pathway of stone, unseen from the ledge above. What adventure scene would you use as a picture of faith? Be as specific as possible.

_____

_____

_____

Faith—believing who God is, what He says and what He does —is vital to the Christian life. It is central to everything we do as Christians—to our daily living, to our spiritual growth and to growing up in Christ.

_____

_____

Is believing in God the same as Indiana Jones's blind leap into nothingness? Explain why you answered yes or no.

_____

_____

Unlike the riddle makers who choreographed Indy's adventure, God doesn't demand blind faith. He doesn't require that we believe in Him without any evidence at all. How has God shown you—in general as one of His people as well as in very personal ways—that He is worthy of your trust?

_____

_____

Jesus became a man and lived among us, and God's prophets spoke specifically about the Messiah who would come. Our faith is firmly based on the solid evidence of the life of Jesus Christ and the truth of God's Word. We didn't have to jump into a bottomless chasm when we named Him Lord and Savior.

Date: _____

The Dimensions of Down-to-earth Faith
(pages 98-104)

Now let's work on bringing faith out of the mystical realm of the spiritual and into the practical, nuts-and-bolts area of everyday living.
• Faith Depends on Its Object—Faith is not simply a matter of believing. It's *what* we believe and *who* we believe in that determines whether or not our faith will be rewarded.

What are some of the things you put faith in every day? Start your list by thinking about who you're trusting when, for instance, you ride in a car or grab a burger at the local drive-through.

_____

_____

Who are some of the people you put faith in every day? You might begin your list with Mom and Dad, teachers at school and your best friend. What are you trusting the people on your list for?

_____

_____

What happens when the object of your faith fails you? How do you feel? What do you think? What happens to your faith? Give several different examples.

_____

_____

_____

How is faith in Jesus different from faith in the objects and people you listed above?

_____

_____

Jesus Christ is the ultimate faith object. The fact that He never changes makes Him totally trustworthy (see Numbers 23:19; Malachi 3:6; Hebrews 13:8). He has never failed to do all that He said He would do or be all that He said He would be. He is eternally faithful.
• The Depth of Faith Is Determined by the Depth of Your Knowledge of the Object—We struggle with our faith in God when our knowledge of Him is insufficient. Faith in God only fails when we misunderstand God and His ways.

As you look back on a time when you were struggling with your faith in God, what didn't you understand about Him? What did you learn about God through that experience?

_____

_____

_____

If you want your faith in God to grow, you must increase your understanding of Him. What are you doing to keep growing in your understanding of God?

_____

_____

The only limit to our faith is our knowledge and understanding of God. That knowledge grows every time we read the Bible, memorize a Scripture verse, participate in a Bible study or meditate on a biblical truth. The potential for your faith to grow as you seek to know God is boundless.

• Faith Is an Action Word—Faith isn't just saying, "I believe." Faith without action is not faith (see James 2:17,18). Faith involves action. Faith makes a move. Faith speaks up.

> Evaluate your faith. Are you a spiritual couch potato—or an active-duty soldier following Jesus' directions? Are you sometimes one and sometimes the other? If so, why? What keeps you stretched out on the couch sometimes or always?

_____

_____

_____

> Now think about your participation in church or youth group. Are you treating it like an infirmary or a military outpost? Why?

_____

_____

_____

> God's people—the Church—exist to be change agents in the world, taking a stand, living by faith and accomplishing something for God. What are you doing to be actively involved in His cause? (Such activity is crucial to a real faith.) What could you be doing to be more actively involved in God's cause?

_____

_____

• "If You Believe You Can, You Can"—Okay, you're not much into poetry, but read the poem one more time anyway. (It's on pages 101 and 102 of the text.)

> When have you seen one or two of the truths of this poem acted out in real life, preferably _your_ life? Be specific.

_____

_____

How is positive believing different from positive thinking?

_____

_____

_____

_____

Positive believing is as valid as the object of faith, which is the living and written Word of God—Jesus Christ and the Bible. With the all-powerful God of the universe as the object of your Christian faith, there's hardly any limit to the spiritual heights that your positive believing can take you.

• "Twenty Cans of Success"—Someone has said that success comes in cans and failure in cannots. And the "Twenty Cans of Success" (pages 103 and 104 in the text) will help expand your knowledge of Almighty God and build your faith.

> Read through the "Twenty Cans of Success" again. Which can holds a truth that has helped you in the past? Describe the situation and how that truth was illustrated.
>
> _____
>
> _____
>
> _____
>
> _____
>
> Think about what's going on in your life right now. Which can do you need to open today? Let that particular truth shape a quick prayer to God!
>
> _____
>
> _____
>
> _____
>
> _____

The quicksand of cannots is not where believers need to dwell, and the "Twenty Cans of Success" will help you climb out of the mire. Open one or more whenever you need them!

Date: _____

WHAT HAPPENS WHEN I STUMBLE IN MY WALK OF FAITH?
(pages 105-108)

Have you ever felt, after an especially extreme stumble and fall, that God is ready to give up on you? Do you ever fear that you've crossed the line and moved beyond the limits of God's love? Then keep reading! These truths are for you!

• God Loves You Just the Way You Are—God's love is not based on what you do or don't do. Read that again: God's love is not based on what you do or don't do.

> What did you learn about God's love from Mandy's discussion with me (Neil)?
>
> _____
>
> _____
>
> _____

> Where in your life have you felt that being loved and accepted is based on what you do or don't do?
>
> _____
>
> _____
>
> _____

God is different from those situations and people you just identified. God loves you not because you are lovable but because it is His nature to love you. God loves you because God is love. And why not read that again, too? Say it aloud: "God loves me not because I am lovable but because it is His nature to love me. God loves me because God is love."

• God Loves You No Matter What You Do—God wants us to do good, of course. But, through His Son, Jesus, God has already made provision for our failures so His love continues constant in spite of what we do.

When have you been able to keep loving someone despite something hurtful he or she did? What did this situation teach you about how God loves you?

_____

_____

_____

When has someone kept on loving you despite something awful, wrong or insensitive you did? What did this situation show you about how God loves you?

_____

_____

_____

God will keep on loving you, no matter what you've done. No matter what you do or how you fail, God has no desire not to love you and accept you completely. Even when you forget who you are as His child and stumble off the path of the Spirit-led life, He still loves you. Again, God loves you simply because it is His nature to love.

Start Stomping!

Get Real!

God's people—the Church—exist to be change agents in the world, taking a stand, living by faith and accomplishing something for God. (Yes, you've read those words before, but they're worth repeating.) Genuine faith is active faith, so let's get real! Come up with a project that you and a friend, or you and some members of your church youth group could do to walk your talk in your community. Is there a soup kitchen you could volunteer at? Do some older folks you know need help with yard work or home and car repairs? Does your church need volunteers in the nursery? Look around and then go accomplish something for God!

You *Can* Do It!

Get a couple of good-sized pieces of paper (and we don't mean wimpy 8 ½ x 11-inch sheets) and cut out two soup cans. Okay. Next step. Earlier you identified a can that has worked for you and a can that you need right now. Write out in your own words, on one of your paper cans, the can that helped. On the other can, write out the can you need. Take the can that worked to a friend or, better yet, to youth group and be ready to share your story and ready to learn from other people's stories. Now you can do one of two things with the can that describes what you need. If you're up to it, share it with someone or several people who will pray for you. If that's just too risky—and it's okay if it is—put your can somewhere that you'll see often so you'll get that truth drilled into your brain and will start living the can.

Snip! Snip! Snip! or an Exercise in (God's) Forgiveness

Maybe a pair of scissors will help you understand what God has done for you and drive home the truth that God loves you just the way you are, no matter what you've done. Cut some 8 ½ x 11-inch paper into 8, 10 or 12 smaller pieces (depending on how big you write). On each of these smaller pieces of paper, write one of the ways you've failed to be the person you know God wants you to be. Write down all the sins you struggle to forgive yourself for. Write down all the ways you've blown it—big time and not so big time. When you've finished, let each one be a brief prayer of confession and renunciation. Then cut the piece of paper into the tiniest pieces possible and throw them away. That sin is gone, forgiven by God completely and forever. Okay? He will never hold them against you. Okay!

> Your love really is pretty amazing, God. You'll love me just the way I am and no matter what I do. That's a pretty good deal for me, and yet sometimes I ignore Your love and do what I want to do instead of what You want me to do. I'm sorry, God. Please forgive me. And please help me learn to trust You more. I need to open those "cans of success" and get to know You better. And, knowing You, I want to get out there and accomplish something for You. Show me what You want me to do and then be with me as I do it. I pray in Jesus' name. Amen.

Strength Givers

These words are *for* you and *about* you! As you read each day's verse, ask yourself, "How would my life be different if I could live out this truth?"—and ask God to help you do so.

The Power of
Positive Believing

Monday—Colossians 3:12

Tuesday—Ephesians 2:10

Wednesday—Romans 8:31

Thursday—1 Peter 5:7

Friday—John 16:33

You Can't Live Beyond What You Believe

You've probably never thought about how much your faith is like driving a golf ball off a tee. But if your faith is off, your walk will be off. If your walk is off, you can be sure it's because you faith is off. And the longer you hold on to a poor belief system, the more "off" your walk will be. So let's take a look at your belief system.

• Belief Quiz—Parts One and Two—If you haven't already, take the two-part Belief Quiz on pages 111 and 112 of the text.

What surprised you about the questions on the Belief Quiz? What kind of questions did you expect?

_____

_____

_____

Why is it important to look at what you believe will bring you success, significance, fulfillment, satisfaction, happiness, fun, security and peace?

_____

_____

_____

If what you believe about these eight values—about success, significance, fulfillment, satisfaction, happiness, fun, security and peace—doesn't line up with what God says about them, your walk of faith will be off to the same degree that your belief is off. Keep that in mind as you work through this chapter and the next.

Date: _____

Feelings Are God's Red Flag of Warning
(pages 112-117)

God desires His children to experience success, significance, fulfillment, satisfaction, happiness, fun, security and peace. But sometimes our ideas about how to achieve these goals are not completely in harmony with God's plans and goals for us, and God can use our emotions to let us know that we may be holding on to a poor goal based on a wrong belief.

• Anger Signals a Blocked Goal—When we feel angry about a relationship or a project, it's usually because someone or something has blocked our goal.

When has anger signaled a blocked goal for you?

_____

_____

• Anxiety Signals an Uncertain Goal—When we feel anxious (worried and afraid at the same time), our anxiety may be signaling our uncertainty about the goal we have chosen.

When has anxiety helped you recognize your uncertainty about a goal you had set for yourself?

_____

_____

• Depression Signals an Impossible Goal—Depression is a signal that our goal, no matter how spiritual or noble, may never be reached. Depression is the expression of hopelessness.

When has depression signaled that you are working towards a goal you have little or no chance of achieving?

Depression resulting from an impossible goal can also be related to a wrong concept of God. What was David's wrong concept of God in Psalm 13?

What did David do to get out of his depression? What truth did he begin to focus on?

If Satan can destroy your belief in God, you will lose your source of hope. But if you can follow David's example and move away from your wrong concept of God to the truth about Him, you will once again find hope.

• Wrong Responses to Those Who Frustrate Goals—When our happiness or success hinges on reaching a goal that can be blocked or that is uncertain or impossible, we may attempt to control or manipulate the people and circumstances that stand between us and success.

How do you tend to respond to people who block your goals? Do you get bitter, angry or resentful? Do you feel sorry for yourself? Do you take charge and become a manipulation master as Darcy did?

Which of the answers to the preceding questions are pleasing to God?

Bad goals can mean bad situations between friends. Unless we adjust our goals, we'll waste months and possibly years living in bitter defeat, hardly the victorious lives God would have us live.

Date: _____

How Can I Turn Bad Goals into Good Goals?
(pages 117-119)

• Good question—but first let's define a good goal.

> In light of what you've just learned about goals from the discussion of anger, anxiety and depression, how would you define a good goal?

> _____

> _____

> _____

If God has a goal for your life, it cannot be blocked; its fulfillment is neither uncertain nor impossible. A good goal, then, is God's goal for you.

> What was God's goal for a young woman named Mary? (See Luke 1:26-38.) And what was Mary's response?

> _____

> _____

> _____

As impossible as God's goal for Mary may have sounded to her (she would give birth to a son while still a virgin and her son would be the Savior of the world!), she responded, "Be it done to me according to your word" (Luke 1:38). And that is to be our response to God's goals for us.

• Knowing the Difference Between Goals and Desires—The secret to achieving God's goals is learning the difference between a godly goal and a godly desire:

A *godly goal* is any specific choice reflecting God's purposes for your life that does not depend on people or circumstances beyond your ability or right to control—and you are the only person you have the ability or right to control. A *godly desire* is any specific choice that depends on the cooperation of other people or the success of events or favorable circumstances you cannot control.

You Can't Live Beyond What You Believe

What are some of God's goals that cannot be blocked? (You can find three on page 119 of the text.)

_____

_____

_____

What can you gain by aligning your goals with God's goals and your desires with His desires?

_____

_____

Darcy would save herself a lot of grief if she changed her goal to make the cheerleading squad into a desire, and set herself the goal of doing her best in the tryouts and remaining a good friend to Brittany no matter what happens. No one can frustrate that goal except Darcy herself.

What realigning can you do? What goals would you do well to change into desires? What godly goals can you replace those with?

_____

_____

_____

When we work toward godly goals, we may have to deal with some disappointments, but we won't have to deal with the anger, anxiety or depression that comes when our happiness or success hinges on reaching a goal that can be blocked or that is uncertain or impossible.

Date: _____

Godly Goals Center on Building Character
(pages 119-122)

God's basic goal for your life is character development: becoming the person He wants you to be. Because it's a godly goal, no one can block it but you—although every day you struggle against the world, the flesh and the devil and their opposition to your efforts to become a godly person.

• Read Romans 5:3-5 and James 1:2-4.

What do Paul and James tell us about the opposition we face from the world, the flesh and the devil?

_____

_____

_____

When have you realized how God has used a trial or tribulation in your life to help shape you into the person He wants you to be?

_____

_____

_____

What do you think God is doing in your character through a current trial or tribulation?

_____

_____

• One of the great things about trials and tribulations is that they reveal wrong goals.

When has a trial or tribulation revealed a wrong goal? Be specific.

_____

_____

Consider the trials and tribulations you are currently facing. What wrong goal might they be pointing to?

_____

_____

_____

You Can't Live Beyond What You Believe

When we're going through a trial or tribulation, God doesn't offer us the kind of quick-fix solutions the world holds out. Instead, He uses those dark, difficult times of testing to bring us to the point of recognizing that we can totally rely on Him and Him alone to meet our needs. And that's a lesson definitely worth learning.

Start Stomping!

World, You've Got to Be Kidding!

Choose one of the eight goals you looked at earlier: success, significance, fulfillment, satisfaction, happiness, fun, security and peace. Then illustrate—with your own drawing, with pictures from magazines, with details from life on campus—what the world says is the way to achieve that goal. How effective are the world's ideas? How long-lasting is the success, significance, fulfillment, satisfaction, happiness, fun, security or peace that the world offers? Then consider God's means to that end. What do you think He wants you to do to achieve that goal? (Don't worry if you're not sure. Just stay tuned for the next chapter!)

The Fires of Life

Grab some orange construction paper and cut out tongues of flame. Use a piece of brown to make the logs that feed the fire. Now, on pieces of white paper, briefly describe those times in your life—those trials and temptations—when you've felt as if you've been in the fire. Where you can, note how God used that situation to teach you to rely more on Him and/or to shape you more into the person He wants you to be. Let those incidents where you can see what God was doing encourage you that He is just as involved in those other as-yet-inexplicable situations.

Story Time

It's not always easy to appreciate what God is doing in us when times are tough. Sometimes it's easier to appreciate the good that God is doing or has done through the hard times that other people have experienced. So get together with someone (a long-time believer like Mom or Dad or a pastor, prayer partner, leader in the church, etc.) who will tell you about a fiery time in life and what God did through that trial. Reviewing that time will probably be as encouraging for the person sharing the story as it is for you!

All this talk about godly goals and godly desires can be pretty confusing. I'm glad You make it clear that the basic goal You have for my life is for me to become the person You want me to be. God, help me to cooperate with that goal. Give me patience and hope when life is hard and doesn't make sense. I need to know that You're using those kinds of times for my good. I know that You're using those times to teach me to depend on You. I want to learn that—but please be merciful as You teach me. I pray in Jesus' name. Amen.

Strength Givers

These words are *for* you and *about* you! As you read each day's verse, ask yourself, "How would my life be different if I could live out this truth?"—and ask God to help you do so.

Monday—Galatians 4:6,7
Tuesday—Romans 8:14,15
Wednesday—Romans 8:17
Thursday—Romans 8:28
Friday—Hebrews 4:16

God's Guidelines for the Walk of Faith

Along your own walk of faith, you'll see—as I (Dave) have—that God uses bad things to produce good results. Yes, it's hard for me to see Davers hurt, but I truly rejoice when I see the Christlike heart of compassion in my little boy.

> When have you seen God use something bad—in your life or in someone else's—to produce good results?

_____

_____

_____

God cries with us when the bad things happen, but He also works to redeem them and make good come from them (see Romans 8:28). If we don't believe in this truth and in God's fundamental goodness, we can become bitter and unhappy. And the devil is more than willing to confuse our beliefs so that we'll grow distant from God. Let's take a look at the beliefs that keep us close to Him.

Date: _____

PROPER BELIEFS LEAD TO A PROPER WALK
(pages 125-136)

If Satan can muddy our minds and weaken our faith with partial truths, he can stop our effectiveness for God and stunt our growth as

Christians. So let's look closely at what the Bible teaches about success, significance, fulfillment, satisfaction, happiness, fun, security and peace. Our beliefs about these things need to be anchored in the Scriptures if we are to walk with Jesus.

• Success Comes from Right Goals—If you ranked yourself low in the success category of the Belief Quiz, you are probably having difficulty reaching your goals in life. And if you aren't reaching your goals, it's probably because you're working on the wrong goals.

> According to 2 Peter 1:5-7, what are seven goals for those of us who call ourselves "Christians"?

> _____

> _____

> _____

> What are the odds for reaching these goals—for achieving moral excellence, knowledge, self-control, perseverance, godliness, brotherly kindness and Christian love? Explain why you answered the way you did.

> _____

> _____

Focusing on God's goals will lead to success in God's terms. As these qualities increase in our lives, we will be useful and fruitful—and that's success!

> Notice what is not mentioned in Peter's discussion of success. No word is said about talents, intelligence or gifts that are not equally distributed to all believers. Why is this significant? Why is this encouraging?

> _____

> _____

Your self-worth is not determined by your talents, intelligence or gifts. Your self-worth is based on your identity in Christ and your growth in character, both of which are equally available to every Christian.

What did you learn from Joshua about success in God's terms?

_____

_____

For Joshua, success hinged entirely on obedience to God—and that should be our pattern, too. When we accept God's goal for our lives and pursue it obediently, we'll become the people God wants us to be—and that's big-time success!

God's Guidelines for the Walk of Faith

• Significance Comes from Proper Use of Time—Significance is a time issue. What is forgotten as time passes is of little importance. What is remembered for eternity is of great importance (see 1 Corinthians 3:14; 1 Timothy 4:7,8).

Consider a typical week. What activities are you involved in that will remain for eternity?

_____

_____

What percentage of your time and energy go to those activities of eternal significance that you just listed?

_____

_____

Read the story Jesus tells in Matthew 25:31-40. What does this parable teach you about which activities are significant?

_____

_____

Are you, like Brian, minimizing the impact you may be making on people for Jesus? Or do you, like many of us, need to refocus your energies so that you are indeed spending time, energy and effort on significant, important, eternal things?

_____

_____

What we do and say for Christ, no matter how unimportant it seems in this world, will last forever. We have His word on that!

• Fulfillment Comes from Serving Others—For the Christian, true fulfillment in life comes when we discover our unique gifts and abilities and use them to serve others and glorify the Lord (see 1 Peter 4:10). Think for a moment about your unique opportunities for ministry.

> How can you serve God in your family—in your role as son or daughter, brother or sister? Be specific! And let the lesson of Matthew 25:31-40 cue you!

> _____

> _____

> _____

> How can you serve God at school and with your friends? These are your mission fields, and you are the person God has appointed to serve there.

> _____

> _____

> _____

Sadly, many people miss their calling in life by looking for fulfillment in the world. Find your fulfillment in the kingdom of God by deciding to be an ambassador for Christ in the world (see 2 Corinthians 5:20).
• Satisfaction Comes from Living a Quality Life—Satisfaction results from living righteously and seeking to make everything we're involved in better. Satisfaction comes from doing our best for God, whatever it is we're doing.

> If you're not super satisfied with your life right now, take the quality/quantity test. Are you trying to do a few things well—or are you doing a lot of (too many?) things and just trying to hang on?

> _____

> _____

> _____

> Apply the quality/quantity yardstick to relationships, too. Are you investing in a few good friendships—or are you spreading

yourself too thin and finding yourself with lots of acquaintances but no solid friend?

_____

_____

_____

What do your answers to the two preceding questions tell you about yourself? What changes in your life do they get you thinking about making?

_____

_____

_____

The key to personal satisfaction is not gaining more responsibilities, but working hard and doing your best in the responsibilities you have. Likewise, personal satisfaction with relationships comes with following Jesus' example and investing in some close and quality relationships with people who will be there when you need them.

• Happiness Comes from Wanting What You Have—The world says that happiness is having what we want, but God says, "Happy is the person who wants what he has."

> Which definition of happiness—the world's or God's—has the greatest influence over you right now? What's resulting from that influence?

> _____

> _____

> _____

> Satan's lie is that God won't give you what you need or enough of what you need. What area of your life is Satan lying to you about? Arm yourself against this attack by reading God's truth in Matthew 6:25-34.

> _____

> _____

> _____

Talk to God about what is blocking your happiness right now. Ask Him to change your focus, your heart and your values so that you can be happy in what He has given you.

You have everything you need to make you happy forever: you have Christ, eternal life and the love of a heavenly Father who has promised to supply all your needs. If you really want to be happy, learn to be thankful for these gifts and everything else God has given you, not greedy for what you don't have.

• Fun Comes from Enjoying Life Moment by Moment—Real fun is hanging loose and enjoying life as it happens, and the secret to enjoying life moment by moment is removing the roadblocks.

Probably the biggest roadblock to Christian fun is our tendency to keep up appearances. Satan wants us to fear what people say and think about us. When has this roadblock been real for you? When have you, like King David, wanted to let loose and have fun but, unlike David, listened to the party poopers in your life and held back?

_____

_____

Think about the last time you had fun. First, was it a big carefully planned event or a spur-of-the-moment activity? Why was it fun? Second, were you afraid of what people would think about you if you let yourself have fun? Why or why not?

_____

_____

What else, if anything, keeps you from having fun? Let God know about these roadblocks to enjoying the gift of life and ask Him to show you how to avoid them and start having more fun.

_____

_____

Fear of what people think moves us to become people-pleasers. Be concerned about pleasing God—and let yourself enjoy the gift of life He's given you!

• Security Comes from Focusing on Eternal Values—The key to experiencing security in our lives is to depend on things that will last for eternity, not just for a time.

What are you depending on? Make a list below and then cross out those things that won't last forever.

God's Guidelines for the Walk of Faith

_____

_____

_____

What does your list—the way it looks now—tell you about yourself? Where will you start looking—and finding—real security?

_____

_____

_____

Security comes only from relating to that which is anchored in eternity, and one of those things is God's love. What does Paul teach about God's love in Romans 8:35-39?

_____

_____

_____

Nothing—absolutely nothing—can separate us from the love of God! Now that's security! So the greatest security you can find comes with taking a firm grip on values and relationships that will endure as long as God Himself.

• Peace Comes from Quieting the Inner Storm—The key to experiencing peace is understanding that it is primarily an internal issue. We already have peace with God (see Romans 5:1), but the peace of God is something we need to turn to every day (see John 14:27).

What does Philippians 4:6,7 teach about the peace God gives?

_____

_____

_____

When have you experienced a peace that passes understanding while the storms of life raged around you?

_____

_____

_____

What storms of life are raging around you now? What can you do—what will you do—to plug into the peace God offers you?

_____

_____

Nothing will happen to you today that God and you can't handle. Your daily time of worship, prayer and reading God's Word will help you find that peace of God you need and want.

Start Stomping!

"Before" and "After"

Have you ever seen those ads for muscle-building drinks or anti-baldness remedies or fat-reducing concoctions? They often have a "before" and an "after" picture to try to convince you of the product's effectiveness. Well, come up with your own "before" and "after" poster illustrating the world's ideas of success, significance, fulfillment, satisfaction, happiness, fun, security and peace versus God's. Focusing on God's message like this will help you ignore the loud but wrong message of the world.

Take a Look in the Mirror

No, we don't mean a glass mirror. We mean the mirror of a friend who knows you well. Get together for a Coke and talk about who you guys are and what gifts God has given each of you. Ask your friend what strengths or talents he or she sees in you—and do the same for your friend. Then brainstorm ways you can use those gifts for God. If you love basketball, can you coach elementary kids at the YMCA after school? If you love kids, can you help out in the three-year-olds' Sunday School class? If you like to write or draw or do office work, can your church use you? Learn about yourself from a friend who knows you well and let him or her help you discover a new mission field!

Iᴛ Sᴏᴜɴᴅs Cᴏʀɴʏ, ʙᴜᴛ...

Count your blessings! Focusing on what we don't have means unhappiness. So focus right now for a few minutes on what you do have! On a piece of paper, race the clock and see how many blessings you can write down in 60 seconds—and I bet that won't be enough time! Look back on this list when the Madison Avenue ad makers, the cliques at school, or Satan himself are making you want more than what you have. On your mark! Get set! Go!

God's Guidelines
for the Walk of
Faith

It makes a lot of sense, God. If I focus on Your goals for my life, I'll surely find success—the kind of success You want me to have. Yep, it makes a lot of sense and it sounds simple enough, but I'm not sure how easy it is to live out. Help me, God, to want for myself what You want for me—moral excellence, knowledge, self-control, perseverance, godliness, brotherly kindness and Christian love. And help me to be obedient to You as I work toward these goals. Thanks for these guidelines You give me for walking a life of faith in You and for giving me the power, through Your Spirit, to keep on walking. I pray in Jesus' name. Amen.

Sᴛʀᴇɴɢᴛʜ Gɪᴠᴇʀs

These words are *for* you and *about* you! As you read each day's verse, ask yourself, "How would my life be different if I could live out this truth?"—and ask God to help you do so.
Monday—1 Thessalonians 1:4
Tuesday—2 Corinthians 5:14,15
Wednesday—Jeremiah 29:11
Thursday—Romans 8:38,39
Friday—Colossians 2:7

Winning the Battle for Your Mind

Perhaps you're like Shelley—spiritually out of touch and defeated in your daily life. You may not realize that Satan is battling to control your mind and ruin your life. May this chapter help you realize that God can renew your mind and free you from the struggle.

Date: _____

GOD'S WAY VERSUS MAN'S WAY

(pages 139-141)

Faith is God's way to live. Trying to think and reason without God is man's way to live. God's way (the high road) and man's way (the low road) are often in conflict.

- Let's consider some of the differences between these two paths.

    First, what do the following passages teach you about the high road versus the low road?

    Proverbs 3:5,6

    _____

    _____

    _____

    Isaiah 55:9

    _____

    _____

Why is the Bible important for walking the high road?

_____

_____

• We walk the low road when we think thoughts and consider plans that conflict with what God's Word says, and doing so can slow our spiritual growth and block our maturity in Christ.

> Remember the example in the text? God's high road is honesty; the low road is cheating. When have you considered and even chosen the low road? What were the consequences of that decision? What did you learn from that incident?
>
> _____
>
> _____
>
> In what area(s) of your life do you tend to consider and even occasionally choose the low road?
>
> _____
>
> _____
>
> _____
>
> What will you do to get your thoughts back on the high road? (Don't worry if you're not sure at this point. That's what this chapter is all about!)
>
> _____
>
> _____

• The Source of the Low Road—The two mains sources of low-road thoughts and ideas are our flesh (the part of us that was trained to live independently from God before we became Christians) and Satan.

> Think again about those areas of life where you feel especially susceptible to low-road thoughts and actions. What is behind that—your flesh, Satan or both?
>
> _____
>
> _____

When have you been able to stand strong in the battle and choose the high road? What were the consequences of that decision? What did you learn from that incident?

_____

_____

You may feel helpless in this battle between the high road and the low road, but in each skirmish you are actually the one who determines which road to walk. Let's work now on a strategy you can use.

Date: _____

Strongholds Are the Prime Target of Our Warfare
(pages 141-146)

• In 2 Corinthians 10:3-5, Paul explains the battle for the mind.

First, Paul states that the battle is not fought by human ability but by "divine power." Why does this make sense?

_____

_____

_____

Second, the main targets that must be destroyed are the "strongholds" in the mind, those bad patterns of thought that are burned into our minds either through repetition over time or through one-time, deeply shocking experiences. What strongholds are you aware of? (We'll look at several in a moment.)

_____

_____

_____

• Our Environment—You and I were born physically alive and spiritually dead in a world opposed to God's design. Before we came to Christ, all our experiences came from this sinful environment, and this environment influenced and shaped us.

What people, places and events have tempted you to travel the low road?

_____

_____

_____

What books, movies and music have tempted you to take the low road?

_____

_____

_____

What painful or even traumatic events (accidents, death, etc.) have drawn you to the low road?

_____

_____

We learned ways (which may or may not have been God's way) to cope with what happened to us and to solve the problems that resulted. When you became a Christian, your sins were washed away, but your old ways of thinking and behaving remained—a stronghold from your environment.

• Temptation—Whenever you feel attracted to the low-road plan instead of God's high-road plan for your life, you are experiencing temptation.

Read Matthew 4:1-11. What temptations does Satan set before Jesus?

_____

_____

_____

What does Jesus do to stand strong against those low-road temptations? What can you learn from His example?

_____

_____

Satan knows just what buttons to push to tempt you away from depending on Christ. He knows where you are weak, and that's where he attacks.

• Consideration and Choice—At the point when we're tempted to take the low road, we are on the threshold of a decision. If we don't immediately choose to "take captive every thought to make it obedient to Christ" (2 Corinthians 10:5, *NIV*), the likelihood of yielding to that temptation increases.

Winning the Battle for Your Mind

Remember the "Cathy" cartoon strip? What happened when Cathy didn't immediately dismiss the tempting thought?

_____

_____

_____

When have you found yourself, like Cathy, hesitating at the threshold of decision and yielding to the low-road temptation? Give an example and say how you wish you would have handled it.

_____

_____

_____

When have you, like the guy in the text tempted toward lust by a pornographic magazine, been able to separate yourself from the source of temptation?

_____

_____

_____

The Bible teaches that God has provided a way of escape from every temptation (see 1 Corinthians 10:13). But the escape is at the threshold—when the thought first occurs.

• Action, Habit and Stronghold—People who study human behavior tell us that if we repeat an act for six weeks, it will become a habit. If we exercise that bad habit long enough, a stronghold (a low-road pattern of thinking) will be established.

What strongholds have formed a groove in your mind? Circle any of these possibilities that apply and add your own.

Hostility

Inferiority

Manipulation

Sexual addiction

Homosexuality

Eating disorders (anorexia or bulimia)

Other: _____

Date: _____

In Order to Win the Battle for Your Mind, You Need a Plan
(pages 146-148)

Negative patterns of thinking and behavior that you've learned along the way don't need to control you.

• You can unlearn anything you've learned, and you can reprogram a mind that has been programmed wrong.

What is the source of the wrong programming in your mind?

_____

_____

_____

Past experiences may have been spiritually or emotionally devastating. What can you do to start getting to know God as your loving Father and yourself as His accepted child? Could Christ-centered counseling help?

_____

_____

_____

• There's more going on in our minds than the bad patterns we've developed. We're also up against the devil.

If Satan can place a thought in your mind—and he can—it isn't much more of a trick for him to make you think it's your idea. Why does Satan disguise his suggestions as our ideas?

David, Ananias and Sapphira fell victim to ideas that Satan planted in their minds. Looking back on times you've stumbled, what idea was probably placed in your mind by Satan?

_____

_____

_____

If Satan can get you to believe a lie, he can control your life—but you can have victory over Satan. By hearing God's Word being taught, studying your Bible and living as Christ's disciple, you can experience God's transforming and healing touch on your life. Let's develop a more specific plan.

Date: _____

Expose the Lie and You Win the Battle
(pages 148-150)

Satan's power is the lie. He has no power over us except what we give him when we don't take every thought captive and hold it up next to God's truth before believing and acting on it.

• Since Satan's primary weapon is the lie, our defense against him is the truth. Before we outline a specific plan of defense, write out the truths of these three passages and personalize them. (For instance, in John 8:32, what bondage will God's truth free you from?)

John 8:32

_____

_____

John 17:15,17

_____

_____

Ephesians 6:14

_____

_____

Now let's look at your part in the battle.
• First, you must be transformed by the renewing of your mind (see Romans 12:2).

> According to the following verses, how do you renew your mind?

> Colossians 3:15

> _____

> _____

> Colossians 3:16

> _____

> _____

You renew your mind by filling it with God's Word.

> What are you doing to give your mind a steady diet of God's Word?

> _____

> _____

As you continue to fill your mind with God's truth, you will become better equipped to recognize the lie and take it captive.
• Second, prepare your mind for action (see 1 Peter 1:13).

> What's the risk of dreaming and fantasizing?

> _____

> _____

What good can come from dreaming and imagining—and what does that good result hinge on?

_____

_____

If you imagine yourself traveling the high road by obeying God's truth, you can move yourself toward living that way. Just be sure to follow through by doing what you imagine.
• Third, take every thought captive and make it obedient to Christ (see 2 Corinthians 10:5).

What does this instruction mean in real life? Be specific.

_____

_____

_____

When have you successfully recognized a thought as counter to God's Word and been able to refuse it lodging in your brain? Let the example (or two or three) you come up with give you strength the next time a thought arises that needs to be rejected.

_____

_____

When a thought pops into your mind that doesn't agree with God's Word, refuse it immediately. Say aloud, "In Jesus' name, leave! I'm a child of God." Choose instead to believe and act on the truth.
• Fourth, turn to God.

What does Philippians 4:6 say?

_____

_____

Why is praying aloud the smart thing to do when your commitment to the high road is being challenged by low-road thoughts from the world, the flesh or the devil?

_____

_____

When we pray, we acknowledge God and expose our thoughts to His truth. Furthermore, as we turn to God, He will do His part. Victory in the battle for our minds is the inheritance of everyone who is in Christ.

Start Stomping!

Construction Zone!

What can you make to remind you to choose the high road of life? If you're good with words, come up with a slogan or write a poem. If you like art, make a poster. If you want something even more hands-on, do a 3-D road. Maybe making a bracelet or a bookmark is more your kind of thing. Whatever you do, put your "high road" wherever it can encourage you to choose that route throughout your day.

Give It Six Weeks and Then...

We've talked about bad thought patterns, knee-jerk reactions and habits that have taken root in your life, and you've learned what to do about those. Now think for a moment about a good habit you would like to develop over the next six weeks (a regular Bible study time, an exercise schedule, a Scripture memorization program, whatever!)—and do a six-week experiment. It just may stick! You've got nothing to lose by trying!

Make It Real

Read Philippians 4:8,9 again and then make it real. If you're a words person, list some specifics to flesh out those categories Paul calls you to think about. If you're more into scissors and glue, make a collage to illustrate things that are honorable, right, pure, lovely, of good repute, excellent and worthy of praise. You'll have an easier time tuning out the world's loud and strong voice if you can quickly replace it with the kinds of thoughts God wants His people to have.

It makes me angry, God, to think that Satan can put ideas in my head and then make me think they're my own. No wonder they call him the deceiver! He's playing hard ball! But I'm glad that, in You, I can have victory in this battle. I'm glad that You give me Your Word so that I can know the truth. I ask You to loosen those strongholds that keep me in bondage. And help me be a more able warrior when it comes to taking my thoughts captive and making them obedient to Christ. It's in His name I pray. Amen.

Winning
the Battle for
Your Mind

Strength Givers

These words are *for* you and *about* you! As you read each day's verse, ask yourself, "How would my life be different if I could live out this truth?"—and ask God to help you do so.

Monday—Colossians 2:11
Tuesday—1 Peter 5:8
Wednesday—Colossians 1:13
Thursday—Ephesians 3:12
Friday—Philippians 4:8,9

You Must Be Real in Order to Be Right

- Is there a little bit of Matthew in you?

    Is your sense of self-worth dependent on your performance in a certain area?

    _____

    _____

    _____

    What do you tend to do with your negative feelings about yourself or about life in general?

    _____

    _____

    _____

    What did you learn from Matthew's experience? What encouragement do you find in his story?

    _____

    _____

Matthew had some wrong beliefs, and when Satan convinced him to stuff his feelings inside, he couldn't discover that those beliefs were based on lies. As soon as Matthew recognized his false beliefs and got rid of them, his depression lifted.

Date: _____

Our Emotions Reveal What We're Thinking
(pages 153-157)

In general, our emotions are a product of our thought life. If we don't think right—if we don't see God accurately and clearly understand His Word—we won't feel right.

• Is there a little bit of Jeremiah in you?

Do you feel as if God is against you? What problems are you seeing Him as the cause of?

_____

_____

_____

Are you feeling trapped by certain circumstances in your life? Are you feeling afraid to trust God to protect you and therefore afraid of what life holds?

_____

_____

_____

At this point, Jeremiah's beliefs about God are off because of the pain he's suffering. God wasn't the cause of his problems—and He isn't the cause of yours. But Jeremiah wasn't thinking right, believing right or seeing his circumstances right, so he wasn't feeling right either.

Look again at Lamentations 3:19-24. What emotions does Jeremiah express here?

_____

_____

_____

What caused the turnaround? What lesson can you learn from Jeremiah?

_____

_____

Once Jeremiah was honest with God about his pain and his feelings, his wrong thinking became right thinking and his emotions followed.
• What You See Is What You Think—We are not shaped as much by what's happening around us as we are by how we view what's happening around us.

Life's events don't control who we are. God determines who we are, and our view of life's events determines how well we handle the pressures of life.

Think about the last event that got you really down on yourself. What was your perspective on that event? Why did your view of that event lead you to feel so bad?

_____

_____

_____

Looking back at that same event, what perspective would have helped you deal with the situation and prevented such negative feelings about yourself?

_____

_____

_____

Although we have very little control over our feelings, we do have control over our thoughts, and our thoughts determine our feelings and how we act. That's why it is so important to fill our minds with knowledge of God and His Word.

Our feelings always react to what we think is true, whether it's true or not! Thinking your parents won't let you buy a car brings out different emotions than realizing the truth that they are going to buy the car for you, doesn't it? What half-truth or full-on lie are you believing about certain circumstances in your life? (Don't hesitate to call on a trusted friend or pastor to help you answer this question.)

_____

_____

Now determine (again, help is allowed and even encouraged!) God's truth about the situation. Think hard about that truth and let that right thinking guide your feelings.

The order of Scripture is to know the truth, believe it, walk according to it and let our emotions be a result of our obedience. When you believe what you feel instead of the truth, you can't help but stumble in your walk of faith.

Date: _____

DON'T IGNORE THE WARNING SIGNS OF YOUR EMOTIONS
(pages 157-161)

Our emotions are to our souls what our physical feelings are to our bodies. Just as physical pain keeps us from more serious injury and infection, anger, sorrow, joy, etc., let us know what's going on inside.

What do you usually do with your feelings?

_____

_____

_____

What attitude toward feelings did you grow up with? Are feelings good? Bad? Just part of being human? What happened to help shape your attitude toward feelings?

_____

_____

Now hear the truth. Feelings are neither good nor bad. They're just part of being human. And just as you respond to the warnings of physical pain, you need to learn to respond to emotional warning signals—and each of us can choose from among the following three options:

• Stuffing Our Emotions—We stuff our emotions when we ignore our feelings. This is the choice not to deal with them.

You Must Be Real in Order to Be Right

According to David's account in Psalm 32:3,6, what happens when we stuff our feelings?

_____

_____

_____

How has your body reacted when you've stuffed your feelings? Have you experienced headaches? Nausea? Sleeplessness? Loss of appetite?

_____

_____

_____

Why do you sometimes choose to stuff your feelings?

_____

_____

_____

What truth about who God is can encourage you to open up to Him about what you're feeling? (See, for instance, Psalm 51:1 and Romans 8:38,39.)

_____

_____

Problems can seem bigger than God, but they never are. Know that truth—and know, too, that bottling up your feelings can hurt you and short-circuit your relationship with God. Stuffing your emotions is not a wise or healthy choice.

• Letting It All Hang Out—Another unhealthy way to deal with emotions is to let them all hang out, telling anybody and everybody exactly how you feel.

When have you lost control of your emotions and exploded with hurtful words and anger?

_____

_____

_____

Was that outburst healthy for you? Why and/or why not?

_____

_____

_____

Was your outburst healthy for those around you? Explain.

_____

_____

_____

What guidelines for dealing with anger does God give in Ephesians 4:26 and James 1:19,20?

_____

_____

_____

Take comfort that the apostle Peter also got into trouble due to unbridled expressions of his feelings. Nevertheless, God used him in the New Testament church, evidence of the kind of powerful change that the Holy Spirit can produce in us.

• Acknowledging Our Emotions—If we go to prayer feeling angry, depressed or frustrated, but pretend to be happy, God isn't pleased. He already knows how we feel. If we're not real, we're not right.

Read again David's prayer for (against!) his enemies in Psalm 109:8-13. What surprises you most about his words?

_____

_____

_____

What comfort do you find from David's honest expression of his feelings? What does his example give you permission to do?

_____

_____

_____

_____

When we are open with God about our feelings, we aren't so much at risk of clobbering ourselves or other people with them.

_____

_____

_____

_____

What emotions do you need to honestly acknowledge before God right now? Take 3 minutes (or 33 minutes) and do so. After all, He already knows exactly what you're feeling—and He loves you anyway!

_____

_____

_____

Being honest with God is crucial to your mental and spiritual health. So is being honest with a trusted friend or two.

With whom can you be totally honest emotionally? Do you let yourself do so? If you're not sure there's anyone in your life right now with whom you can be emotionally honest, make that a topic of prayer. Ask God to help you take the risk of trusting your feelings to someone—and ask Him to bring that person into your life.

Paul and even Jesus Himself modeled having a few intimate friendships with people who can help you through the emotions and struggles of life's hard times. Don't hesitate to follow their examples. Be open and honest with God and with one or two trusted friends. It's crucial for your mental health.

Date: _____

EMOTIONAL HONESTY: HOW TO DISH IT OUT AND HOW TO TAKE IT
(pages 161-165)

We can acknowledge that emotional honesty is important, but living out that truth is not always easy. It's not always easy to be honest, and it's not always easy to deal with another person's honesty.

• One of our challenges in the area of emotions is learning to respond to others when they honestly tell us their feelings.

Do you shy away from people in pain because you worry about not having the right words? What does my (Neil's) experience (pages 161-162 of the text) tell you?

_____

_____

_____

When has someone come alongside you in your pain and cried with you? What did that action mean to you?

_____

_____

_____

What specific acts of kindness have encouraged you when you've gone through hard times?

_____

_____

_____

Words aren't the important issue when someone is experiencing great inner pain. We shouldn't respond to their words; we should respond to their pain (see Romans 12:15).

• While it's challenging to deal with other people's emotional honesty, we also face challenges when it comes to being emotionally honest ourselves. Here are some guidelines.

1. When it comes to acknowledging emotions, honesty is the best policy—but speak the truth in love (see Ephesians 4:15).

2. Know your limits and give yourself permission to delay making a decision or talking through an issue until you've calmed down emotionally.

3. Recognize that a lot of physical factors (hunger, tiredness, hormones) affect your emotional limits.

You Must Be Real in Order to Be Right

Which truth have you learned the hard way in life?

_____

_____

_____

Which guideline do you most need to work on?

_____

_____

_____

What will you do the next time you have emotions you want to share honestly with someone? Who is someone trustworthy of your honesty? Thinking through the possible scenario ahead of time can help you act the way you want to—and the way God wants you to!

_____

_____

The important process of renewing your mind includes acknowledging your emotions honestly and expressing them in love. Dealing with your emotions properly is an important step in keeping the devil from gaining a place in your life.

START STOMPING!

WHAT YOU THINK IS WHAT YOU FEEL

Still trying to get a handle on the fact that emotions follow thoughts? It's true, and recognizing that fact may keep you from becoming your own worst enemy as you deal with the ups and downs of life.

Practice seeing the thoughts-precede-emotions pattern with these three scenarios.

The cashier at McDonald's can't even crack a smile and seems to growl when asking whether you want fries with your burger. What thoughts lead you to feel down on yourself? To feel compassion for the cashier?

You'd studied hard for the biology test but the questions seemed to be from a different chapter, if not an entirely different book. What thoughts cause you to beat yourself up mercilessly? What thoughts help you accept the results and strive to do better next time?

The relationship had been going well—at least that was your perspective. What thoughts lead to depression? What thoughts lead to sadness rather than a total lack of self-worth?

It's Not Just For Trains

Get with a friend and blow off steam! That may mean playing a game of one-on-one basketball, or going for a hard run, or (fill in the blank) _____ . God won't mind what you do as long as you don't hurt yourself or anyone else. He already knows what's inside!

Random Acts of Kindness

Who in your life needs some kindness today? Someone who's having a bad day? Someone who's received the fallout from some of your "emotional honesty"? (First apologize and ask for forgiveness. Then be kind!) Someone who serves behind the scenes and could use a pat on the back? Someone in your family whom you'd rather tease than be nice to? Choose a person and a random act of kindness for each day of the week. (For ideas, consider who that person is, but also look above at your answer to the question, "What specific acts of kindness have encouraged you when you've gone through hard times?") But be warned. This kind of behavior can be gratifying to the point of addiction!

> I guess it shouldn't surprise me that You who made me
> and who gave me my emotions don't mind hearing
> about them. I guess I'm relieved, God, to learn I don't
> have to hide from You or pretend to be something I'm

not. It seems awkward to be angry or depressed or frustrated or irritable with You, but I know You can help me deal with those things. Teach me to be honest with my emotions—and to be loving when I am. Help me learn to listen to my emotions and understand what they're telling me. And, God, give me a friend who will accept me and all my crazy emotions—and help me be that kind of friend, too. I pray in Jesus' name. Amen.

You Must Be Real in Order to Be Right

STRENGTH GIVERS

These words are *for* you and *about* you! As you read each day's verse, ask yourself, "How would my life be different if I could live out this truth?"—and ask God to help you do so.

Monday—Colossians 3:4
Tuesday—Galatians 3:26,28
Wednesday—Ephesians 4:15
Thursday—Ephesians 4:26
Friday—Romans 12:15

Healing Emotional Wounds from Your Past

• Look again at the story of Cindy and Dan (pages 168-169 of the text).

> What misunderstanding of Romans 8:28 did Cindy have?
>
> _____
>
> _____
>
> What did I (Neil) explain to Cindy—and you—about God's promise in that verse?
>
> _____
>
> _____
>
> What truth (it's a recurring theme in this book!) did Cindy need to get a grip on before she could be free of the crippling effect of being raped?
>
> _____
>
> _____

Jesus Christ, not our past hurts, determines our identity. When Cindy learned that, she was able to move on from the rape and serve the Lord. Are you still working on learning that lesson? The next few pages can help.

Date: _____

Bad Things Do Happen to Good People
(pages 169-170)

All of us have a number of hurtful, upsetting experiences in our past that have scarred us emotionally. And one or more of the events may have caused deep inner pain that has hindered your growth as a Christian.

> What bad things have happened to you?
>
> _____
>
> _____
>
> _____

> What feelings do you still have as a result of one or more of the events you listed?
>
> _____
>
> _____
>
> _____

We're calling these long-term feelings, which hide deep inside you, *primary emotions*, and their power is determined by our past experiences. The more painful the experience, the more powerful the primary emotion. And anything in the present that links you with your past experience can trigger those primary emotions.

> What can trigger the primary emotions you listed above—certain words, situations, smells, topics of conversation, dates, locations, activities, etc.?
>
> _____
>
> _____
>
> _____

We can't completely isolate ourselves from triggers, so we need to learn how to resolve past hurts.

Date: _____

Learning to Resolve Primary Emotions
(pages 170-172)

We have no control over a primary emotion when it is triggered—so don't feel guilty when those emotions arise.

• True thinking about the trigger can help you deal with the emotions you're feeling as a result of that trigger.

When has someone (like the football player talking to his meathead teammate) helped straighten out your thinking when emotions were overwhelming you?

_____

_____

_____

What kind of right thinking can you arm yourself with in anticipation of experiencing once again the primary feelings you know are lurking inside?

_____

_____

_____

• Think for a moment about how you are coping with serious hurts in the past.

Which options have you chosen or are you choosing?
_____ You have no conscious memory of the pain.
_____ You avoid people or experiences that bring back bad memories.
_____ You remember what happened but act like it never did.
_____ You try to cover up the pain with food, drugs or sex.
_____ Other: _____

God is light. What does He want us to do with pain from the past?

_____

_____

God knows our hidden hurts, and He knows that His light—His love, His truth, His power—can bring healing to those hurts. If those dark areas are beyond conscious memory right now, trust that God will bring them to light at the right time.

Date: _____

SEE YOUR PAST IN THE LIGHT OF WHO YOU ARE
(pages 172-173)

God gives us two guidelines when it comes to resolving the painful experiences of the past. First, look at those experiences in light of who you are now as opposed to who you were then.

Why is this a good guideline for resolving pain from the past?

_____

_____

What truth does God give you in 2 Corinthians 5:17 to help you follow this guideline?

_____

_____

_____

How have you resolved the question, "Where was God when all this was going on?"

_____

_____

"Where was God when all this was going on?" is a fair question to ask God—He knows you're thinking about it anyway. As you ask this question and wait for an answer, accept the truth that God was with you when others hurt you or when you made some bad choices. Beyond that, let the answer be a mystery this side of heaven.

What can God do for you in the present despite the deep hurts of the past?

Healing Emotional Wounds from Your Past

_____

_____

God is in your life right now desiring to set you free from your past. You can't fix your past, but you can let God set you free from it. Seeing past events through your identity in Christ is what starts the healing, freeing process.

Date: _____

Forgive Those Who Have Hurt You in the Past
(pages 173-180)

The second step toward resolving the painful experiences of the past is to forgive those who have hurt you.
• But why should you forgive the one(s) who hurt you? Let's look at three reasons.

First, forgiveness is required by God. What does Jesus teach in Matthew 6:14,15?

_____

_____

_____

Second, forgiveness is necessary to avoid being trapped by Satan (see 2 Corinthians 2:10,11 and Ephesians 4:26,27). How can Satan use our lack of forgiveness to trap us and cause greater pain and suffering?

_____

_____

Third, forgiveness is to be the normal way of life for all Christians. Why do we Christians need to be forgiving people?

_____

_____

Forgiveness frees us from the past. Forgiveness keeps our relationship with God open. And forgiveness needs to characterize all our relationships because all of us need forgiveness.

• What Is Forgiveness?—In order to understand what forgiveness *is*, we must first see what it is *not*.

List two or three things that forgiveness is not and circle those that are new to you.

_____

_____

Forgiveness is not forgetting. Forgiveness is not putting up with someone's sin; it isn't being a doormat or continually allowing yourself to be hurt by another. And forgiveness is not revenge or a demand for repayment.

Forgiveness means deciding to live with the consequences of another person's sin (something you're doing whether or not you forgive the one who hurt you). What is freeing about this definition? What freedom will you find if you decide to live with the consequences of another person's sin?

_____

_____

_____

You can choose to live in bitterness and unforgiveness or, by deciding not to hold the offense against the offender, in peace and forgiveness. The latter, of course, is God's way.

• Twelve Steps to Forgiveness—We don't truly forgive someone without admitting the hurt and hatred involved. But until you forgive, you will continue to be hurt because you have not released yourself from the past. Forgiveness is the only way to stop the pain, and here are 12 steps you can walk through to forgiveness. Let's look at them closely.

1. Write on a sheet of paper the names of the persons who hurt you.

Why do you think it is important to be specific?

_____

_____

_____

Why is it wise to get God involved in this step?

_____

_____

_____

Why do you and God probably need to be on this list of people you need to forgive?

_____

_____

2. Face the hurt and the hate.

It's not a sin to admit the reality of your emotions. In fact, why is it healthy to write down how you feel about these people and their offenses?

_____

_____

3. Realize that the cross of Christ makes forgiveness possible, fair and right.

Why is this important fact crucial for your journey to forgiveness?

_____

_____

4. Decide that you will bear the burden of each person's sin (see Galatians 6:1,2).

Write what this step means in your own words—and explain why it is key to true forgiveness.

_____

_____

5. Decide to forgive.

What does this step suggest about the relationship between feelings, the will, and actions when it comes to forgiveness?

_____

_____

6. Take your list to God and pray the following: "I forgive (name) for (list the offense[s])."

Why is it important not to rush through this step?

_____

_____

7. Destroy the list.

What does this step represent?

_____

_____

8. Do not expect that your decision to forgive will result in major changes in the other persons.

Whom will your decision to forgive have the greatest impact on? Why?

_____

_____

What are we called to do regarding those people we are forgiving?

_____

_____

9. Try to understand the people you have forgiven.

What do you know about the people who have hurt you that helps you understand that they have been hurt, too?

_____

_____

_____

Healing
Emotional
Wounds from
Your Past

Why is this an important step to take toward freeing yourself from bitterness?

_____

_____

10. Expect positive results of forgiveness in you.

What are some of the positive results that can come with extending forgiveness to those who have hurt you?

_____

_____

11. Thank God for the lessons you have learned and the maturity you have gained as a result of your decision to forgive the offenders (see Romans 8:28,29).

What lessons can be learned from forgiving those who have offended you? And why is forgiveness a step toward maturity?

_____

_____

12. Be sure to accept your part of the blame.

What action often needs to follow accepting responsibility (see Matthew 5:23-26)?

_____

_____

_____

• Forgive and Be Free—Forgiveness really can heal the hurts of the past.

> Read again the account of Corrie ten Boom facing a guard from her Nazi concentration camp (pages 178 and 179 of the text). What message did God have for you personally in this story?

> _____

> _____

When we forgive, we throw off the chains of bitterness and start the process of healing emotions that have been damaged. When we have forgiven the people who have hurt us, we find that we have really set ourselves free.

Start Stomping!

Live and Learn

Bad things do happen to good people. Bad things do happen to God's people. Talk to someone who has walked with God a long time, through good times and bad. Ask that person to share what God taught him or her through those bad times. Ask that brother or sister in the Lord what he or she has learned along the way about forgiveness and the freedom that comes with forgiving.

A Picture Is Worth...

You've read a lot of words about bondage to pain from the past and the freedom that comes from forgiveness. Make that contrast more real for yourself by drawing a picture, writing a poem, creating a collage, fashioning a sculpture, putting a new tune together—anything that will help remind you in a tangible way the transformation from bondage and darkness to freedom and light that is available when we obey the command to forgive. (Like all of God's commands, this one is given for your benefit!)

Take a Walk

Review the 12 steps to forgiveness and start walking. This path will indeed take you to the point where the pain from the past no longer has a hold on you. You will probably always remember the incident, but the intense emotion will be gone. It's a gift of grace from God who heals. These 12 steps show you how to receive that gift.

God, this forgiveness stuff is a tall order! I'm glad You're by my side to help me walk the path I need to walk to be free from the pain of the past. Please be at work in my spirit to make me want to forgive. Give me the strength I need to choose to forgive. And, as You did for Corrie ten Boom, transform my heart so that I can reach out—at least in prayer—to those who have hurt me. And as I walk this path to forgiveness, make me very aware of all that You've forgiven me for and all that You continue to forgive me for, and may that awareness motivate me to give to others the kind of forgiveness You have given to me. I pray in Jesus' name. Amen.

Healing
Emotional
Wounds from
Your Past

STRENGTH GIVERS

These words are *for* you and *about* you! As you read each day's verse, ask yourself, "How would my life be different if I could live out this truth?"—and ask God to help you do so.

Monday—Matthew 6:14,15
Tuesday—Romans 8:1
Wednesday—Galatians 5:1,13-15
Thursday—1 Corinthians 2:12
Friday—Colossians 3:1-4

CHAPTER
TWELVE

Dealing with Rejection in Your Relationships

Everyone knows what it feels like to be criticized and rejected at times, even by the very people in our lives we desperately want to please.

> What experiences and people come to mind when you hear the word "rejection"?
>
> _____
>
> _____
>
> How do you usually deal with rejection?
>
> _____
>
> _____
>
> How would you like to be able to deal with rejection?
>
> _____
>
> _____

God Himself rejected us until we were accepted by Him in Christ at salvation (see Romans 15:7). Since then we have been the target of Satan, the accuser, who never stops lying to us about how worthless we are to God and others.

What role do you think Satan plays in the feelings of rejection you live with? Why would he want you to focus on feelings and experiences of rejection?

_____

_____

_____

In this life we all have to live with the pain and pressure of rejection —but we don't have to let them cripple us or our growth in Christ.

Date: _____

WHEN YOU ARE CRITICIZED OR REJECTED
(pages 182-186)

We have several options when it comes to dealing with rejection, but unfortunately we all learned early in life to take one of three defensive (and ineffective) positions.

• Beat the System—Some people defend themselves against rejection by buying into the dog-eat-dog system and learning to compete and scheme to get ahead.

Are you dealing with rejection by trying to earn acceptance through your performance? Are you driven to do everything right? Are you unable to let anyone get close to you? Are you worried and stressed out most of the time?

_____

_____

_____

Even if this isn't your defensive position of choice, evaluate the effectiveness of this option. Why does or doesn't it work?

_____

_____

_____

How can this "beat the system" approach impact a person's relationship with God?

_____

_____

Beat-the-system controllers are some of the most insecure people you'll ever meet. And, sadly, their defensive strategy only leads to more rejection. Others soon resent these people for their self-centered living.

• Give in to the System—Many people respond to rejection by simply giving in to it. They continue to try to satisfy others, but their failures drive them to believe that they really are unlovable and that being rejected makes sense.

Where, if at all, are you buying into someone's false judgment of your worth? Which of the world's false values lead you to self-condemnation and feelings of inferiority?

_____

_____

_____

Even if this isn't your defensive position of choice, evaluate the effectiveness of this option. Why does or doesn't it work?

_____

_____

_____

How can this "give in to the system" approach impact a person's relationship with God?

_____

_____

By giving in to the world's false judgment, people who accept the world's standards of worth and realize they don't measure up can only look forward to more and more rejection. In fact, having bought the world's lie, they even reject themselves, leading them to question or doubt any acceptance that might come their way.

• Rebel Against the System—Rebels and dropouts respond to rejection by saying, "I don't need you or your love." Although deep inside they crave acceptance, these people refuse to admit their needs.

Are you a rebel or a dropout when it comes to dealing with rejection? Do you feel a lot of self-hatred and bitterness and often wish you'd never been born? Are you irresponsible and undisciplined, rebelling against everyone and everything despite the fact that you're hurting yourself by doing so?

_____

_____

Even if this isn't your defensive position of choice, evaluate the effectiveness of this option. Why does or doesn't it work?

_____

_____

_____

How can this "rebel" approach impact a person's relationship with God?

_____

_____

The attitude and behavior of people who rebel tend to alienate others and push them to defend the system being rejected. The rebels' responses to those who reject them breeds further rejection.

• Defensiveness Is Defenseless—As long as we live on this earth we will experience rejection. How should we respond to it? Should we try to defend ourselves? No—for two reasons.

First, if you are in the wrong, you don't _have_ a defense. What happens—as hard as it may be to do—when you simply respond to an accusation with, "You're right; I was wrong"?

_____

_____

_____

Second, if you are right, you don't *need* a defense. What does Jesus model for you in this regard? See 1 Peter 2:23.

_____

_____

If you find yourself responding to rejection defensively, try focusing your attention on those things that will build up and establish your faith.

What are some specific things—things that can build up your faith—you can think about the next time you feel rejected or unworthy?

_____

_____

The world's system for determining your value as a person is not what determines your value. Your allegiance is to Christ your Lord, not to the world, and He is the reason you are worthy.

Date: _____

When You Are Tempted to Criticize or Reject Others
(pages 186-193)

Rejection is a two-way street: you can receive it and you can give it. We've looked at the first. Now let's look at how to respond to the temptation to tear up others with criticism or rejection.
• First, what message does God have for you in these two passages?

Romans 14:4

_____

_____

Philippians 2:3

_____

_____

Think about your relationships for a moment. Are you in line with what God's Word says in Romans 14:4 and Philippians 2:3? Or do you tend to attack people's character rather than taking responsibility for your own? Do you tend to be absorbed with your own needs instead of looking out for your friends' needs? What do you need to confess and repent?

_____

_____

Instead of devoting ourselves to developing our own characters and meeting each other's needs, we often yield to Satan's prodding to criticize each other and selfishly meet our own needs. We need to practice what God's Word says if we are to grow up in Christ and glorify Him in our friendships.

• Focus on Responsibilities—Satan has deceived us in our relationships by tempting us to focus on our rights instead of our responsibilities.

Think about your relationship with your parents. What happens when you focus on your rights? What happens when you focus on your responsibility to be an obedient son or daughter? (If you can't answer this second question, find out!)

_____

_____

Now think about your relationship with a friend. What happens when you focus on your rights? What happens when you focus on your responsibility to be the kind of friend to your friend that you want him or her to be to you? (Yes, that's a loose paraphrase of the Golden Rule.)

_____

_____

Keep in mind that God is more concerned about how well we fulfill our responsibilities, not whether we receive everything we feel we have coming to us.

• Don't Play the Role of Conscience—Sometimes we may be tempted to play the role of the conscience or even the Holy Spirit in someone else's life.

Why is being another person's conscience sometimes tempting?

_____

_____

_____

How do you feel when someone plays conscience for you?

_____

_____

Our job as God's representatives on this planet is to surround people with acceptance and let the Holy Spirit do His job of convicting in His time.

• Discipline Yes, Judgment No—We are required by God to confront and restore Christians who have clearly violated Scripture (see Matthew 18:15,16), but we are not allowed to judge their characters.

How would you react to "You're a liar," a statement about your character? To "You just told a lie," a statement about your behavior? Why would you react differently?

_____

_____

_____

Do you tend to confront? Judge? Or avoid the issue entirely? What would God have you do—and how?

_____

_____

We must care enough about people to confront their sinful behaviors, but we should never tear down their characters.

• Express Your Needs Without Judging—It's okay to express your needs to others, but it's important to do so without slamming them in the process.

How do you respond to a "you" accusation ("You never call.")?

_____

_____

How do you respond to an "I" message ("I miss it when you don't call regularly.")?

_____

_____

Think about your own speech patterns. Which is more common—the "you" accusation or the "I" message? How do people respond to your pattern?

_____

_____

We all have basic human needs to feel loved, accepted and worthwhile. The bases for Satan's work of temptation in your life are real needs that are not being met.

What makes it tough for you to express your needs in a proper way?

_____

_____

What need(s) would you share and allow other people to meet if you were willing to take the risk of stepping out from behind your mask?

_____

_____

What's the worst thing that could happen if you took that step of risk? Could you survive?

_____

_____

What's the best thing that could happen if you told someone

what you really need right now? Is that possible result worth the risk?

By not letting other believers meet our legitimate needs, we are acting independently of God and leave ourselves vulnerable to the world, the flesh and the devil. We are also robbing people of the opportunity to minister to our needs.

When have you had the opportunity to minister to someone in need?

What did you feel like when you were able to help? That's the gift you give when you are open and willing to let someone help you!

God works in our lives through committed Christian relationships. So the next time you're tempted to find character defects and performance flaws in another believer, ask for the grace of God to see beyond those externals. After all, isn't that what you want others to do for you?

START STOMPING!

YIKES! WHO'S THAT IN THE MIRROR?

What did you learn about yourself from your study of Romans 14:4 and Philippians 2:3? To whom do you need to apologize? Choose one person on your list and do it today! As part of your apology, you may want to let him or her know that you're learning about what God wants in our relationships with others.

THE "I'S" HAVE IT

What will you say in the following situations? (Practicing "I" messages just may help one pop out the next time a "you" accusation would fly!)

At the last minute, your friend once again cancels plans with you to be with his or her girlfriend or boyfriend instead.

Your mother comments on what you're wearing as you're heading out the door and it feels like criticism.

Your dad focuses on your C+ in math instead of the English grade you worked hard to pull up.

What Have You Got to Lose?

It feels pretty good to have God love you through His people, so dive in! Be wise in whom you choose, but find someone to tell about a need you have right now. Get together with the person before seven days go by. And give yourself permission to start the conversation with, "This is really hard for me...." Don't be surprised when God richly blesses you with warm acceptance and love. That's just the kind of God He is!

> God, You've clearly shown me what You want from my relationships with other people—and I've seen how easy it is for me to be critical instead of taking responsibility for myself. I've also seen how self-centered I can be. Please forgive me—and please change me! Give me, I ask, the grace to not be defensive when I'm rejected, the grace to express my needs without judging the people who are letting me down, and especially the grace to see people as You see them. I guess what I'm saying is "Help me live by Your Golden Rule." I ask that in Jesus' name. Amen.

Strength Givers

These words are *for* you and *about* you! As you read each day's verse, ask yourself, "How would my life be different if I could live out this truth?"—and ask God to help you do so.

Monday—Matthew 7:12
Tuesday—Galatians 6:2
Wednesday—Ephesians 4:1
Thursday—Hebrews 3:1
Friday—1 John 3:11,16

People Grow Better Together

Have you ever thought about Christianity as a team sport? Alone we can easily get discouraged on our Christian walk, but together we find strength as we encourage each other, pray for each other and build each other up.

When has a team of believers helped you through a hard time? How did the believers show they cared? What support did they offer you? And, shifting from the receiving end, what did you do to contribute to the functioning of the team and the well-being of other team members?

_____

_____

_____

If you've never been part of a team of believers—a youth group, a church—what's keeping you back? Busyness? No driver's license? Wanting to be cool or ot wanting to be a nerd? Be honest with yourself about your reasons—and listen carefully for what God wants for you.

_____

_____

A church youth group is a place where you can share your concerns, a place where people really care about you and a place where you and your Christian friends can help each other grow as disciples of

Jesus Christ. A church youth group is the place for you if you're serious about your faith.

Date: _____

Discipleship: The Heartbeat of Growth and Maturity
(pages 196-197)

Discipleship is the intensely personal activity of two or more persons helping each other experience a growing relationship with God. And such caring and growing together is what being Christ's disciples is all about.

• You are both a disciple and a discipler in your Christian relationships.

In what relationship(s) are you more the disciple than the discipler? What have those relationships helped you learn?

_____

_____

_____

In what relationship(s) are you more the discipler than the disciple? What have you learned in those relationships?

_____

_____

_____

• You also have the opportunity to be a peer counselor and to receive counsel in your Christian relationships.

When has God guided you through the counsel of a fellow believer? Be specific.

_____

_____

_____

_____

When has God used you to offer His truth to someone in need of counsel? What did you learn from that experience?

_____

_____

As a believer, you are disciple as well as discipler, counselor as well as counselee. The following designs for discipleship and concepts for counseling offer some practical guidelines for your ministry to others.

People Grow Better Together

Date: _____

Designs For Discipleship
(pages 197-204)

In Colossians 2:6-10, Paul outlines three levels in the ministry of discipling others. Each step of the way, sin, the world, the flesh and the devil can interfere. These points of conflict must be resolved and replaced by specific steps of growth.

• Level 1: Identity—Here, people establish and come to understand their identity in Christ (see Colossians 2:10).

What does the person being discipled need to learn in each of the following areas of life in order to establish his or her identity in Christ?

Spiritual life

_____

_____

Mind

_____

_____

Emotions

_____

_____

Will

_____

_____

Relationships

_____

_____

If you are now working to establish your identity in Christ, which area(s) would you like help in? Whom can you go to for discipling? Ask your youth pastor for suggestions.

_____

_____

If you feel solid about your identity in Christ, think back to who helped you get to this point. Whom can you thank? And whom can you help disciple? Let your youth pastor know of your willingness to be a discipler.

_____

_____

• Level 2: Maturity—At this level, believers become mature in their faith and are "built up in [Christ]" (Colossians 2:7).

What does the person being discipled need to learn in each of the following areas of life in order to become more Christlike?

Spiritual life

_____

_____

Mind

_____

_____

Emotions

_____

_____

Will

_____

_____

Relationships

_____

If you're confident about who you are in Christ and now are working to become more mature in your faith, which area(s) would you like help in? Whom can you go to for discipling? Ask your youth pastor for suggestions.

_____

_____

Even if you've been a believer for a while, you may still be working on some of these areas. Which ones would you like some discipling help in? For which areas could you be a discipler? Talk to your youth pastor about both your needs and your willingness to minister.

_____

_____

Many new Christians want to know right away, "What should I *do* to grow as a Christian?" when the better question is, "Who should I *be*?" Keep in mind that people (yourself included) can't behave as mature Christians (Level 3) until they have matured as Christians (Levels 1 and 2).

• Level 3: Walk—Level 3 discipleship involves supporting people in their daily walks (see Colossians 2:6).

What characterizes the spiritually mature person in each of the following areas?

Spiritual life

_____

_____

Mind

_____

_____

Emotions

_____

_____

Will

_____

_____

Relationships

_____

_____

_____

Think about your home, your school, your youth group and society in general. Where in these areas do you need help functioning more like a believer? To whom can you go for discipling and prayer support?

_____

_____

Immature believers don't need to constantly be told what they should *do*. Instead, let's celebrate with them what Christ has already *done* and help them become who they already are in Him. Amen? Amen!

Date: _____

CONCEPTS FOR COUNSELING
(pages 205-210)

If you have a compassionate heart and a knowledge and love of the Lord, God can use you to encourage and instruct young people with problems. The goal of such counseling is to help people experience freedom in Christ so they can move on to maturity and fruitfulness in their walks with Him. Here are five practical tips:

• Help People Identify Root Issues—Psalm 1:1-3 compares the mature Christian to a fruitful tree. The fruitfulness of the branches above the ground is the result of the fertility of the soil and the health of the root system that spreads into it.

People Grow
Better Together

How can this image help you if someone comes to you for counseling? What does this image encourage you to address?

_____

_____

What are some of the emotions and situations that can prompt someone to seek Christian counseling?

_____

_____

For each item you listed above, write a possible root cause for the primary emotions touched by the situation (rejection, fear, unforgiveness, false belief system, rebellion).

_____

_____

What has this discussion of root issues helped you understand about yourself?

_____

_____

• Encourage Emotional Honesty—People are generally willing to share what has happened to them, but they are not usually willing to share their failures or how they feel about them.

With whom do you have an easy time being emotionally honest? Why?

_____

_____

_____

What can you do to encourage a person you're counseling to be emotionally honest? Consider your body language, your verbal responses, the setting of the conversation, etc.

_____

_____

• Share the Truth—When Christians seek advice or counsel, it's usually because their problems have caused them to think there is something wrong with them. They may feel that God can't possibly love them.

When have you had such feelings? How did you deal with them? Be specific.

_____

_____

Based on your own experience and what you've learned in *Stomping Out the Darkness*, what will you do for someone who comes to you feeling something's wrong with them and God can't love them?

_____

_____

• Call for a Response—Your role in advising and counseling your friends is to share the truth in love and pray that the person will choose to accept it.

Why is prayer key to any counseling situation? Give two or three reasons.

_____

_____

Why is the fact that you cannot choose change for your friend (only your friend can do that!) freeing news to you as the counselor?

_____

_____

• Help Them Plan for the Future—Sometimes when we're in the depths of despair, the future can look pretty bleak.

What truth can you offer someone feeling overwhelmed by problems and despair?

People Grow
Better Together

_____

_____

_____

What practical steps can you encourage that person to take? More specifically, what kinds of supportive relationships will you propose? What will you teach about the difference between goals and desires (see chapter 7)?

_____

_____

You and I are what we are by the grace of God. All we have and can hope for—as disciplers and disciples, as counselors and people in need of counsel—is based on who we are in Christ. May your life and your ministry therefore be shaped by your devotion to Him and the conviction that He is the way, the truth and the life.

Start Stomping!

Try It! You'll Like It!

God calls us as individuals to follow Him, but He wants us to do so in a community. So if you're not plugged into a Christian community, make it your goal to find a youth group within the next few weeks. You need the group—and the group needs you. If you're already involved in a youth group, take a step toward greater involvement. That can mean anything from behind-the-scenes service to the group to an up-front leadership role. God has just the place for you!

Your Tree of Life

Look again at the diagram on page 207 of the text. The top tree reflects a barren life; the bottom, a fruitful life. Now draw your own tree. What root problem(s) are you dealing with? What food does your root system need? What instruction would you benefit from? In what areas of your life (spiritual life, mind, emotions, will, relationships) do you need encouragement and challenge (i.e., discipling)? Where do you need to do some pruning? Having answered these questions, develop a plan for taking care of your tree. Consider whom you can ask for help with the gardening. In other words, who would you like to disciple you? Also figure out where you will go to get the nurturing (true belief system, acceptance, forgiveness, freedom, submission) that you need to bear fruit. Keep in mind, too, that prayer is like oxygen for your tree of life.

A Prayer For All of Us

Whether you're in need of Christian support and counsel right now or it's your turn to offer that kind of support and guidance, this prayer is for you: "God, grant me the serenity to accept the things I cannot change, the courage to change the things I can, and the wisdom to know the difference." Put these words to music, write them on a poster, etch them onto a piece of metal or burn them into wood, draw a picture representing serenity, courage and wisdom—whatever you do, make this prayer a part of your life.

> God, thank You that I can live out my faith as a part of a team. There are times when I realize I just can't do it alone—and I realize I never would have come to know You without Your people reaching out to me with Your love. Thanks for all the folks You've placed in my life to help me learn more about You and help me become more like Your Son. And thank You for the privilege of being able to help others who are at a different place in their Christian walks. Whether it's my turn to disciple or be discipled, to offer counsel or receive it, may I do so in the solid knowledge of Your love, Your light and Your truth. Thank You that I am Your child—and thank You for sending Your Son to make that possible. It is in His name I pray. Amen.

Strength Givers

These words are *for* you and *about* you! As you read each day's verse, ask yourself, "How would my life be different if I could live out this truth?"—and ask God to help you do so.

**People Grow
Better Together**

Monday—John 15:15

Tuesday—Ephesians 2:19

Wednesday—1 Corinthians 15:10

Thursday—2 Corinthians 5:18,19

Friday—Galatians 3:26; 4:6

MORE RESOURCES FROM

NEIL ANDERSON AND FREEDOM IN CHRIST MINISTRIES TO HELP YOU AND THOSE YOU LOVE FIND FREEDOM IN CHRIST.

Books

REGAL BOOKS

Victory over the Darkness
Living Free in Christ
Stomping Out the Darkness (Youth)
Setting Your Church Free
Helping Others Find Freedom in Christ

HARVEST HOUSE PUBLISHERS

The Bondage Breaker
The Seduction of Our Children
Winning Spiritual Warfare
Daily in Christ
The Bondage Breaker Youth Edition
A Way of Escape
To My Dear Slimeball (Richard Miller)

THOMAS NELSON PUBLISHERS

Released from Bondage
Walking in the Light

CROSSWAY BOOKS

Spiritual Warfare (Timothy M. Warner)

STUDY GUIDES

REGAL BOOKS

Victory over the Darkness Study Guide
Stomping Out the Darkness Study Guide

HARVEST HOUSE

The Bondage Breaker Study Guide
The Bondage Breaker Youth Edition Study Guide

TEACHING RESOURCES

REGAL BOOKS

Breaking Through to Spiritual Maturity (Group Study)
Busting Free (Youth Study Guide)